Due
Diligence

Prentice Hall
FINANCIAL TIMES

In an increasingly competitive world, we believe it's
quality of thinking that gives an edge. An idea that opens
new doors, a technique that solves a problem, or an
insight that simply helps make sense of it all.

We work with leading authors in the fields of
management and finance to bring cutting-edge thinking
and best learning practice to a global market.

Under a range of leading imprints, including
Financial Times Prentice Hall, we create world-class
print publications and electronic products giving readers
knowledge and understanding which can then be
applied, whether studying or at work.

To find out more about our business and professional
products you can visit us at www.financialminds.com

For other Pearson Education publications, visit
www.pearsoned-ema.com

PEARSON
Education

Due Diligence

Definitive steps to successful business combinations

Denzil Rankine, Mark Bomer
and Graham Stedman

Prentice Hall
FINANCIAL TIMES

an imprint of **Pearson Education**

London • New York • Toronto • Sydney • Tokyo • Singapore • Hong Kong
Cape Town • New Delhi • Madrid • Paris • Amsterdam • Munich • Milan • Stockholm

PEARSON EDUCATION LIMITED

Head Office:
Edinburgh Gate, Harlow, CM20 2JE
Tel: +44 (0)1279 623623
Fax: +44 (0)1279 431059

London Office:
128 Long Acre, London WC2E 9AN
Tel: +44 (0)20 7447 2000
Fax: +44 (0)20 7447 2170
Website: www.business-minds.com

First published in Great Britain 2003

ISBN 978 0 273 66101 6

British Library Cataloguing in Publication Data
A CIP catalogue record for this book can be obtained from the British Library.

10 9 8 7
10

Typeset by Pantek Arts Ltd, Maidstone, Kent.
Printed and bound in Great Britain by Ashford Colour Press Ltd, Gosport.

The Publishers' policy is to use paper manufactured from sustainable forests.

About the authors

Denzil Rankine is chief executive of AMR International, a London-head quartered strategy consultancy and Europe's leading specialist in commercial due diligence. Denzil studied law at the University of Kent and then, after two years with R K Carvill in reinsurance broking, moved into consultancy. In 1983 he joined PBD, a small business development research consultancy specializing in helping British companies enter the US market. Over the following four years he played a leading role in growing the business.

In 1987 Denzil was invited to join the Seer Group, management. He founded the strategic research consultancy division, which worked alongside the corporate finance group. Under his guidance, Seer became one of the first consultancies to offer a specialized commercial due diligence service.

Denzil is author of *A Practical Guide to Acquisitions* (Wiley), *Commercial Due Diligence* (Financial Times Prentice Hall) and *Why Acquisitions Fail* (Financial Times Prentice Hall).

Mark Bomer is a corporate finance partner with BDO Stoy Hayward in London, and he specializes in providing financial due diligence and related services for cross-border transactions. Mark trained with BDO in London and in 1991 he moved to BDO in Paris where he set up BDO's Paris corporate financial department, and where he specialized in providing advice to UK, US and other non-French buyers of French companies. Mark regularly speaks and writes on international financial due diligence and on more general aspects of doing business between the UK and France.

Graham Stedman specializes in corporate and technology law and is experienced in mergers and acquisitions, takeovers, corporate finance, venture capital and corporate reconstructions as well as structuring joint ventures, investment consortia and other collaboration arrangements. He regularly advises on IT contractual arrangements and the protection and enforcement of computer-related intellectual property rights. He has extensive experience of the key issues involved in due diligence programmes. Graham has authored books on the subjects of takeovers, shareholders' agreements and computer contracts. He is recommended in The Legal 500 for his work.

Contents

Part 2: Financial due diligence

Part 3: Legal due diligence

Appendices

Introduction

Why bother with due diligence?

In 1988 Ferranti acquired the American business, International Signal Controls (ISC). Ferranti was a substantial and longstanding UK company, and its acquisition of ISC was to prove the principal cause of its downfall a couple of years later. Ferranti's bankruptcy marked a turning point out of which today's due diligence practices were born.

Later in Chapter 5 we look at Ferranti's acquisition of ISC in more detail, and we conclude that this disaster could have been avoided if Ferranti had conducted a proper due diligence investigation of ISC.

In the 1990s many companies made numerous and substantial acquisitions. In some cases these ambitious acquisition programmes are coming back to haunt their protagonists. Think of the difficulties of Tyco, which acquired some 700 companies in three years, or of Vivendi, or of several high-profile telecommunications businesses.

These are, of course, some of the really well-known examples, involving household names and vast sums of money. But much less well-known businesses could be cited as well, and we look at many examples of smaller acquisitions to illustrate our arguments in this book.

Mergers and acquisitions are big business. In 2001, for example, the total value of acquisitions completed worldwide was €1.8 trillion, representing nearly 29,000 deals – and that was just the disclosed deals, and in a difficult year.

Household names and billions can be at stake; equally for a small family business, to make an acquisition is often critical to its future. An ill-conceived acquistion can easily spell absolute disaster; a successful acquisition can take a business to a new plane completely. The stakes are usually high therefore, and so getting an acquisition right matters a great deal.

We look at some of the ways in which companies can improve their chances of making successful acquisitions. This book shows how a thorough set of due diligence investigations can improve the decision making process by:

- comprehensively testing, reviewing and revising the acquisition strategy;
- minimizing the risk associated with acquisitions;
- securing the best possible negotiating position for a buyer, so improving the terms on which a deal is made.

It is not only prior to completion of an acquisition that due diligence can prove invaluable: before entering into many other major transactions or contracts it can be highly beneficial as well.

With an appropriate acquisition process, including proper due diligence, a prospective buyer can increase the chances of making only the most suitable acquisitions and on good terms. And for deals which do complete, proper due diligence should pave the way for a smooth and effective integration of the new subsidiary following the acquisition, so maximizing the benefits of the deal, maximizing profits, in other words.

And, as we discuss below, it is not only prior to completion of an acquisition that due diligence can prove invaluable: before entering into many other major transactions or contracts it can be highly beneficial as well.

When in the acquisition process should one perform due diligence?

The prime aim of this book is to look at how due diligence can be of great value in the acquisition of a business. We consider how due diligence contributes to the decision of whether or not to proceed with a deal at all, and we show how due diligence can help a buyer to maximize profits flowing from an acquisition, whether by improving the terms of the deal itself, or by anticipating the key issues of post-acquisition integration.

For a due diligence investigation to be meaningful, it must be conducted before a buyer is committed to a deal. Figure 1 illustrates the typical process of an acquisition.

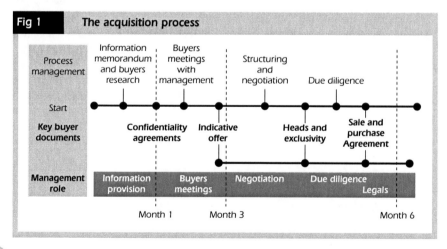

Fig 1   The acquisition process

The main due diligence investigation should usually be conducted after the signature of Heads of Terms or a similar document, the key terms of which are binding on neither party. At this stage the two parties have reached an outline agreement, so there is a deal in principal which justifies the buyer's expenditure on the due diligence investigations. The

> **It is worth noting that this acquisition process is typically Anglo-Saxon. The relationship between buyer and seller is a dynamic mix of shared and opposed interests.**

buyer's due diligence will then allow him/her to test thoroughly the proposition of completing the deal, broadly in accordance with the conditions set out in the Heads of Terms. But, in the light of the results of the due diligence, the buyer might decide to renegotiate these conditions – which, of course, only makes any sense because the Heads of Terms are not binding. Or the results of the due diligence may lead the buyer to withdraw completely.

It is worth noting that this acquisition process is typically Anglo-Saxon. The relationship between buyer and seller is a dynamic mix of shared and opposed interests. With respect to information on the target company it is in the buyer's interest to have access to maximum information before being bound to complete the deal; precisely the reverse of the seller's interest, which is to give as little as possible away before the buyer is committed. Different countries resolve this conflict in different ways. In the UK, for example, the process is typically as outlined above, with the buyer able to conduct full due diligence before becoming committed. In some continental European countries the conflict is typically resolved more in the seller's favour, with the buyer having to commit on the basis of a less thorough investigation. This is one of the many difficult issues arising on cross-border acquisitions where differing local practices come face to face. We look at some of these issues in more detail in this book.

Other occasions when due diligence may be required

Due diligence is primarily associated with the acquisition of a business. But there are other occasions when due diligence can add much value and reduce risk. Before entering any major transaction it is worth considering whether due diligence should be carried out. Examples of such transactions include:

- entering into a joint venture agreement;
- granting a loan;

- investing in the shares of a company;
- entering into a major agreement with a supplier or a customer;
- starting a new business or entering a new market.

In all these cases it can be crucial to be thoroughly well informed before entering into the transaction contemplated. The contents of this book will also be applicable to these kinds of transaction – the thought process behind any due diligence investigation is always similar: the aim is to obtain high-quality and comprehensive information before negotiating and making a committment to a major transaction.

Different kinds of due diligence

This book concentrates particularly on three areas of due diligence: *commercial, financial, legal*.

These are the three main types which will most often be addressed prior to making an acquisition, but other areas may be covered as well. We touch briefly on environmental issues, on pensions and on information technology. For some transactions these and other topics may become key: for instance, information technology will probably be vital to a travel agency, and environmental issues will matter greatly in the acquisiton of a chemical plant.

There is usually a close relationship between financial and commercial due diligence. Indeed, it may sometimes appear that a financial due diligence report covers most of the commercial issues. In fact, commercial and financial due diligence are distinct processes, although they do seek to answer some of the same questions. The critical difference is that a commercial due diligence investigation is based primarily on information available outside the target company, while a financial due diligence investigation is based primarily on documents obtained from the target and on interviews with its management.

The critical difference is that a commercial due diligence investigation is based primarily on information available outside the target company, while a financial due diligence investigation is based primarily on documents obtained from the target and on interviews with its management.

The commercial and financial investigations therefore compliment each other in arriving at the ultimate goal, which is a view on the likely future performance of the target business.

Legal due diligence ensures that the bases of the conclusions of the commercial and financial due diligence investigations are sound: it ensures that the future prospects of the target have a secure legal base. For example, the legal due diligence might ensure that the target has appropriate rights over key intellectual property, that appropriate supplier and customer contracts are in place, that appropriate employment contracts are in place, that the target complies with all legislation relevant to its current and planned activities, that there are no major disputes in progress, and so on.

Legal due diligence might ensure that the target has appropriate rights over key intellectual property, that appropriate supplier and customer contracts are in place, that appropriate employment contracts are in place, that the target complies with all legislation.

It should be clear that it is vital that the commercial, financial and legal due diligence teams co-ordinate their efforts closely. Each team may come across information of great importance to the work of the others. For instance, there is little point in the legal team making a thorough check of the rights to a brand if the business plan is to stop using that brand.

Who performs due diligence?

In this book we concentrate on due diligence that is typically performed by specialist advisers instructed by an acquirer. It is also usual for an acquirer to conduct some of its own due diligence at the same time. The acquirer's own team would usually concentrate on areas which it is particularly well-placed to investigate. Typically, this will include the areas most particular to the acquirer's business activity; it may also cover areas particular to the acquiring company itself – for instance, the acquirer should be best placed to ascertain the extent to which its own business can benefit from operational and other synergies following an acquisition.

As for the external advisers, it is always important that an acquirer's own due diligence team keep in close contact with other due diligence teams, so that knowledge can be shared and each team's work can continually be adjusted in the light of new information.

As for the external advisers, it is always important that an acquirer's own due diligence team keep in close contact with other due diligence teams, so that knowledge can be shared and each team's work can continually be adjusted in the light of new information.

Why should a buyer subcontract any of the due diligence work? Why not do all the investigation work in-house? There are several reasons, including:

- Conducting a due diligence investigation (as this book will make clear) is a specialist skill and much can be gained by using advisers who spend all their time conducting this type of work – specialists will do the work more quickly, are more likely to dig out hidden information, and will have more experience of investigating thoroughly whilst minimizing disruption to the target company.

- Except for very large companies, acquirers simply do not have the resources necessary for carrying out intensive investigations.

- Typically, a buyer will need to concentrate on the big picture, and will need to avoid too much detail. In subcontracting most of the due diligence work a buyer will usually improve its ability to focus on the really important issues.

To future success

We have enjoyed writing this book and hope that you will enjoy reading it. Above all, we would like to think that business managers fresh from reading this book would not commit an error comparable to Ferranti's purchase of ISC!

We feel confident that, in drawing on the ideas and arguments in this book, business owners and managers will be better placed to undertake only the right acquisitions, and on good terms, and that these newly acquired businesses will then contribute substantially to the success of their new owners.

PART 1

Commercial due diligence

What is commercial due diligence?

Commercial due diligence is the process of investigating a company and its markets. It employs information from the target company and secondary sources including published market information, but it also relies heavily on primary sources – customers, competitors and other market participants. The key skills required include the abilities to conduct these interviews effectively, to analyse the industry and to tie all the information to the company's competitive position and to its business plan. Commercial due diligence is one of the most powerful ways to reduce the risk in a transaction; it should also help in negotiating the best deal and planning post-acquisition integration actions.

Commercial due diligence typically takes place in the context of a proposed change of shareholding in a business, i.e. in the context of an:

- acquisition;
- MBO/MBI;
- joint venture.

Commercial due diligence is also used to validate major investments, such as capital investments or investments in a new product or a market entry into a country. In addition, it is a very useful tool to assess a new strategic partner or distributor. Some vendors have found that they would have been better off conducting commercial due diligence on their own subsidiaries before putting them up for sale, allowing them to identify hidden value or problems before the acquirer does. Acquirers who have conducted detailed commercial due diligence on a target can end up with a better understanding of the target's market and competitive position. This then gives the acquirer an upper hand in negotiation.

How does CDD differ from other forms of due diligence?

Commercial due diligence differs from the other main types of due diligence – and particularly from financial and legal due diligence – more in how it is conducted than in what it aims to do. Both commercial and financial due diligence attempt to understand the strengths and weaknesses of the company in order

Commercial and financial due diligence differ in the sources used and the methods employed, and this means that they produce different types of information and insight.

to assess whether a proposed acquisition, investment or divestment should proceed. But they differ in the sources used and the methods employed, and this means that they produce different types of information and insight.

People carrying out financial due diligence focus internally and their information sources are historic. They analyse the financial records of the company in great detail, and speak at length with the company's management – especially the financial management. They may also talk to some outsiders, such as the company's auditors, and with the following winds of professional confidence this is often a valuable source of information.

The focus of commercial due diligence, by contrast, is largely external to the company itself. After some contact with management, it usually starts with secondary sources, such as desk research, and carries on to use primary sources – enquiries among people who are actively involved in the market or who observe it closely. It addresses customers, distributors, specifiers, regulators, suppliers, competitors, new entrants and former employees.

An excellent customer fit is always a good start point for an acquisition. This is not just so that the buyer can cross-sell, but it also means that the buyer understands how to deal with that group of customers. It is therefore un-

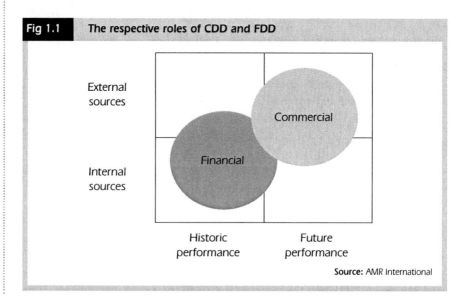

Fig 1.1 **The respective roles of CDD and FDD**

External sources

Commercial

Financial

Internal sources

Historic performance

Future performance

Source: AMR International

surprising that early forms of commercial due diligence were in fact enhanced customer referencing exercises.

Commercial and financial due diligence are complementary activities and the two work programmes should be co-ordinated. Their work will culminate in jointly agreed forecasts. The two teams should communicate freely with each other. They each have access to sources and to information which can be valuable to the other. One simple example is that the financial due diligence team has easy access to lists of former customers and perhaps former employees. The commercial due diligence team could obtain this information as well, but it would take longer.

> **One simple example is that the financial due diligence team has easy access to lists of former customers and perhaps former employees. The commercial due diligence team could obtain this information as well, but it would take longer.**

Similarly, the commercial due diligence team can obtain a more precise view of market size, segmentation and future growth rates than accountants; the financial due diligence team can plug this information into its own forecasts and scenarios. If the teams carrying out commercial, financial and the other types of due diligence operate in concert, this opens up new lines of enquiry and explores uncertainties more effectively.

Later we will address the question of who should carry out a commercial due diligence exercise. Although there are acquirers and investors who conduct commercial due diligence in-house, most of this chapter follows general practice and assumes that the work will be done by a team of external consultants.

Why carry out commercial due diligence? **2**

Reducing risk

The primary reason for carrying out commercial due diligence – as with the other forms of due diligence – is to reduce the risk in a transaction.

Why are acquisitions and other forms of investment so risky and what can be done about it? When one company buys another it is generally buying the right to own its future profit flows, and the risk is that the future performance of the company will fall below the forecasts on which the price of the business is calculated. To compound the problems, the transaction itself can destabilize the company, the integration actions can be disruptive and the hoped-for benefits may not materialize.

> The transaction itself can destabilize the company, the integration actions can be disruptive and the hoped-for benefits may not materialize.

Commercial due diligence provides a thorough understanding of the company's markets and the factors which determine its future performance in those markets. That understanding is an essential part of any assessment of the risks and the value of the business.

An input to valuation

Valuing a company is a notoriously black art. As there is no single best method, a combination of approaches is usually employed. Discounted cash flows are widely regarded as one of the most robust methods, but they depend on the quality of the estimates of the cash flows the business will generate. A detailed commercial due diligence programme can provide these estimates by analysing the future performance of each business unit – and, if need be, going so far as to analyse and forecast the prospects of each individual product line.

The commercial and financial teams need to co-ordinate their efforts and produce a combined forecast. The commercial team will comment on sales growth and margin drivers; the financial team takes the work down to the bottom line.

Commercial due diligence can also contribute to other, less rigorous valuation methods, such as return on investment, net assets or price-earnings ratios. In each case a view of market developments and the company's ability to compete can inform the judgment of the valuation team.

Case study – Sodastream

Cadbury Schweppes decided to dispose of Sodastream, the home-mixed carbonated drinks company, in 1997. The business was non-core and was performing poorly due to difficult market conditions. Home-mixed carbonated drinks had fallen from fashion and the brand was struggling to retain its position on UK supermarket shelves. Germany was a large and growing market for Sodastream, but the company had a difficult relationship with its sole distributor limiting growth prospects.

Numerous potential suitors turned down the opportunity to acquire Sodastream. Then Graphite, a mid-market private equity investor, decided to buy the company, despite the seemingly unpromising market outlook. But first, Graphite commissioned commercial due diligence to verify the company's market position and to justify its valuation. The vendor imposed a tight timetable and only two weeks were allowed for the investigation.

The commercial team spent little time analysing the softdrinks market; Sodastream had only a tiny share and given its closely defined niche, it was hardly competing with the major brands. The team quickly moved on to interviews with customers in the distribution chain – wholesalers and supermarkets in the UK and a range of wholesalers, supermarkets and health stores in Germany.

The team found that Sodastream retained a reasonably strong position in the UK and that management had successfully relisted Sodasteam in some major retailers from which it had been pushed out. In Germany it quickly transpired that Sodastream was a near-fad product in the health niche. Germans on a health-kick wanted to drink more carbonated water, and one large health store chain was pushing its own flavours as mixers. However, due to the poor distributor relationship, machines were in very short supply; one reseller even had a photograph of consumers queuing to buy the machines at a particular store which had a stock. The commercial team went on to discover that one distributor was reselling imported Sodastream machines, although it did not have a relationship with the official sole distributor for Germany.

The commercial team raised this point with Sodastream management. Top managers then admitted that due to the poor relationship with the German distributor, they were encouraging four UK wholesalers to supply a grey market in Germany. Having never been asked about it before, management had not seen the need to discuss this grey channel either with its parent company or potential buyers.

The implications of this information were substantial. First, the UK market was smaller that originally thought as some UK sales were in fact German sales; as the UK market was in decline this meant that there was less retraction to worry about. Second, the German market was larger than originally thought; with its higher margins and strong growth this made the business more attractive. Third, the grey export route was inefficient, Sodastream was only selling its products at the lower UK prices; resolving this inefficiency led to an immediate bottom line improvement.

Graphite went on to acquire the business. Just over a year later a trade buyer approached it and Graphite resold the business for around three times the purchase price.

Lessons learned: a seemingly unattractive business in a seemingly unattractive market can make an excellent investment if the commercial analysis of the company and the market show that the business can benefit from growth in its niche, or an operational improvement. Forecasts in the information memorandum or business plan are often optimistic, but they can be surpassed; this is particularly true if the seller is not very close to the business unit which it is selling.

Showing the red light

As an acquisition proposal is tabled, discussed and analysed within the acquiring company, it builds up a momentum of its own. Once the offer has been put to the vendor, agreed in principle, and all the negotiating and investigating machinery has swung into action, that momentum becomes a powerful force. By this time a number of people – some of them senior within the acquiring company – have invested significant amounts of time and energy (not to mention personal credibility) in getting the proposal this far. In some cases private equity investors and corporate finance advisors are incentivized by deals done,

Showing the red light can be one of the most important functions of the due diligence teams.

not by their ultimate performance. Also deal fever can be fuelled if the press gets wind of the deal and announces it before it happens.

At this point, it takes a brave person to stand up and question the logic for the deal, or point out any grave difficulties within the target company or its market. This can be easier to do for someone who is not a member of the company, although it can still be unpleasant to be the messenger of bad or unwanted news.

Nonetheless, showing the red light can be one of the most important functions of the due diligence teams. Commercial due diligence can reveal information which causes the whole deal to be reconsidered and perhaps postponed or cancelled. Such information could include:

- deteriorating trading conditions in key market segments;
- imminent market or technological changes which will reduce demand for some of the company's major products or services;
- a major new competitor considering market entry, with grave implications for market share and margins.

Of course, the commercial investigations should focus on the key concerns first, so that if the deal is to be stopped, this decision is taken sooner rather than later. A cancelled deal is a major disappointment to those people who have laboured on the process. But a deal which is completed and then fails to deliver at least most of the benefits envisaged can damage and even destroy both companies and careers.

Improve your negotiating power

As every experienced negotiator knows, the better your information, the better your negotiating position. The information provided by commercial due diligence can significantly enhance the buyer's negotiating power. The following two examples show this.

Example 1

A well-run niche service business in conference-centre management was the target for an acquirer. The target company had produced a series of sparkling financial results, the customers held it in high esteem, and the staff were impressive and enthusiastic. Then AMR discovered – simply by talking to a range of customers and potential customers – that the company had referred a small number of enquiries to what seemed to be a rival. It transpired that this rival business was owned by the brother of one of the target company's founders.

The acquirer diplomatically revealed this discovery to the target's management, who immediately agreed to terminate this arrangement and provide appropriate legal undertakings. The interesting development which followed was that a significant amount of extra information began to flow from the target company: it seemed to decide that there was no point in restricting access to information, and that the best policy was to be as open and helpful as possible.

Example 2

A safety equipment business was put up for sale by its owner, a multinational. A market investigation led us to contact a member of its staff who decided that by helping with the enquiries he could improve his prospects following any acquisition. He was soon nicknamed 'Deep Throat' because some of the information he provided included detailed insights into difficulties within the business. Once checked against a range of other sources for exaggeration, this information was used in negotiation and it led to a substantial renegotiation of the price.

Planning for integration

Acquiring companies almost always pay a premium for taking control of a business. That premium can normally be justified only by combining the skills or assets of the acquired company with some part of the acquirer. In reality a surprising number of companies are acquired and then poorly, or half-heartedly, integrated into the other activities of the new parent. In some cases there are good reasons for this. Certain groups encourage operational independence and achieve benefits from combined head-office functions and purchasing power. However, in most cases failed or poor integration results from an overoptimistic view of how close the companies' competences and cultures are, and a failure of planning and management action.

This process of integration should be carefully planned and should start as early as possible – that means way before the acquisition is completed. Too many acquirers turn up at the company headquarters the day after completion and then try to work out the detail of what they should do with their new prize.

As soon as a deal is announced, uncertainty sets in both within the company and among its suppliers and its customers. That uncertainty can be very destructive. Talented staff begin to look around for alternative employment just in case there is no role for them in the new business. Customers seek alternative sources of supply in case the new business raises prices, cuts quality, reduces supply or deletes critical product lines. Competitors will also react aggressively to the move and target customers or even staff.

Ill-planned and consequently poorly executed integration is one of the main reasons for the failure of acquisitions.

This uncertainty is to be avoided. It is also essential to avoid hasty decisions based on an imperfect understanding of the business. It is therefore imperative to have an integration plan prepared in advance. The information and understanding generated by the commercial due diligence process should contribute to the integration plan, particularly the external or market-facing actions.

This may appear to be a counsel of perfection. An acquisition is a frenetic process in which there seems never to be enough time to complete all the essential tasks, never mind those which can be put off until later, but ill-planned and consequently poorly executed integration is one of the main reasons for the failure of acquisitions.

Conducting commercial due diligence

Whether to conduct commercial due diligence

I t is only since the late 1990s that a dedicated commercial due diligence exercise has become standard on most transactions. Almost all large transactions (roughly £50 m and over) now have an associated commercial due diligence exercise, although this can appear in the form of a strategy review or detailed market review. Mid-market transactions (£5–50 m) mostly have commercial due diligence, although their use is higher in deals backed by private equity rather than in corporate transactions. Small deals (up to £5 m) do not always have formal commercial due diligence as the acquirer does not always believe that the cost can be justified, although the cost of commercial due diligence is typically lower than that of legal or financial due diligence.

> Small deals (up to £5 m) do not always have formal commercial due diligence as the acquirer does not always believe that the cost can be justified, although the cost of commercial due diligence is typically lower than that of legal or financial due diligence.

It is neither necessary nor advisable to carry out full commercial due diligence on every single acquisition or investment. Since the main purpose of the exercise is to reduce risk, there is little point in doing so if there is little risk involved. As a rule of thumb, the amount of risk involved depends on the scale and complexity of the transaction and the amount of information which is already available.

The risk of buying a small company which is not far from start-up, and whose price is low, may be relatively minor. If the acquirer is buying its closest competitor, it may have enormous amounts of information about the target already. Management may know each other, and the companies may be serving exactly the same customers and sourcing from the same suppliers. In such cases the commercial due diligence review is often already done in the minds of management and the whole exercise ends up being passed over.

Acquisitions where the size of the acquired company is less than 5% of the size of the buyer stand less chance of success than deals where the proportion is between 5% and 25%.

The case for avoiding commercial due diligence altogether is rare, however. Small deals can be as dangerous as larger ones; the AMR International survey[1] referred to previously has shown that acquisitions where the size of the acquired company is less than 5% of the size of the buyer stand less chance of success than deals where the proportion is between 5% and 25%. There are two main reasons: very small acquisitions frequently receive too little attention and resources, and the entrepreneurial spirit for which the target companies were much admired before the deal can be crushed by the reporting requirements and other disciplines of a larger group.

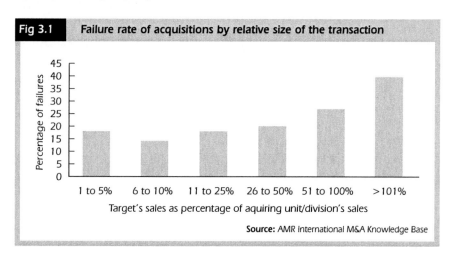

Fig 3.1   **Failure rate of acquisitions by relative size of the transaction**

Percentage of failures (y-axis: 0, 5, 10, 15, 20, 25, 30, 35, 40, 45)

Target's sales as percentage of aquiring unit/division's sales (x-axis: 1 to 5%, 6 to 10%, 11 to 25%, 26 to 50%, 51 to 100%, >101%)

Source: AMR International M&A Knowledge Base

Acquisitions in which overlap between the two companies is total are rare. Obviously in these cases you need to analyse how the combined businesses will perform. In a typical 'horizontal' acquisition you may compete directly with the target in its main markets, but it may have other activities about which you know next to nothing. For example, AMR reviewed one business where the acquirer expected to divest the non-core activities as soon as the deal was completed. It transpired that those activities had been starved of resources and neglected by the group which was being acquired to the point that it was bet-

---

[1] Reasons for the success and failure of aquisitions, based on 350 aquisitions in the UK, France and Germany.

ter for the acquirer to dedicate some resource to turning them around before selling them. This decision was taken only once the acquirer was satisfied that it had sufficient resources and that this unexpected opportunity was within its core competences. In other words, the acquirer satisfied itself that keeping the non-core business would not be an expensive diversion.

When to conduct commercial due diligence

Strictly speaking, the term commercial due diligence should only be applied to an investigation which follows the signing of the Heads of Agreement.[2] This document records an agreement to negotiate the purchase of a business, usually for an approximately agreed price, dependent on the outcome of the various forms of due diligence and the final negotiations.

> Strictly speaking, the term commercial due diligence should only be applied to an investigation which follows the signing of the Heads of Agreement.

Once the Heads of Agreement is signed, there is normally a deal-driven timetable. It usually allows four to eight weeks for the entire due diligence process. However, many acquirers conduct or commission a preliminary review of the opportunity before this stage. This has a number of advantages. First, a preliminary commercial investigation allows an acquirer to base its initial offer on more than basic financial information. This is particularly useful in auction processes. Also, conducting a thorough due diligence exercise is a time-consuming and expensive process. If there are fundamental problems with a company or its markets, you can save a great deal of time and money by discovering them before the full panoply of investigative work is commissioned.

Another advantage of carrying out some investigative work before entering into negotiations with the target is that enquiries can be made unfettered by the restraints imposed by the target's owners, management or advisers. It is, however, now less common for vendors of companies – and particularly the investment bankers who represent them – to seek to impose unreasonable

---

[2] Between different countries there are differences in both terminology and procedure in this area. The USA has a similar document to the UK's Heads of Agreement called a Letter of Intent. In certain continental European countries the Heads of Agreement is virtually a binding agreement to purchase at the specified price, so any meaningful commercial due diligence has to be carried out before it is signed. In the rest of this discussion, reference is to UK practice.

restrictions on the nature and the extent of the enquiries which a prospective buyer can make during the formal period of due diligence.

Example

The chairmen of two quoted groups, both with a medical devices division, met for dinner. One indicated that his group's vital signs monitor subsidiary would be available for acquisition; this was an excellent fit with the other group whose strategic plan included development in this market. Nonetheless, the potential acquirer launched a pre-exclusivity commercial investigation before agreeing to embark on formal negotiations.

The pre-exclusivity commercial review included discussions with the potential target's key customers as well as industry observers and some competitors. It transpired that customers were dissatisfied with the capabilities and performance of the vital signs monitors. They were also frustrated by the company's weak R&D. Competitors confirmed that the potential acquisition candidate was falling behind its competitors. Clearly the seller wanted to find a buyer for an under-performing company. The potential buyer was disappointed with the result, but wasted no further resources on the potential opportunity.

A final word about the timing of the commercial due diligence exercise. If you only begin to investigate the company and its markets in any depth after you have completed the deal, you are too late!

The commercial due diligence process

4

Overview

Commercial due diligence should be run as a project within the due diligence process. Other due diligence projects start simultaneously or slightly later and are run in parallel. A typical CDD project is shown in Figure 4.1.

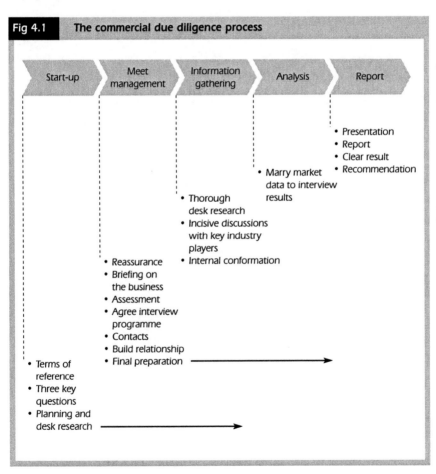

Fig 4.1   The commercial due diligence process

Start-up · Meet management · Information gathering · Analysis · Report

- Presentation
- Report
- Clear result
- Recommendation

- Marry market data to interview results

- Thorough desk research
- Incisive discussions with key industry players
- Internal conformation

- Reassurance
- Briefing on the business
- Assessment
- Agree interview programme
- Contacts
- Build relationship
- Final preparation

- Terms of reference
- Three key questions
- Planning and desk research

Establish the terms of reference

The need to establish the terms of reference may seem so obvious that it is hardly worth mentioning, but this is where CDD exercises can start to go astray. The CDD team should be aware of the full circumstances of the deal and team members should be given clear guidance towards the key issues. CDD should not be conducted in a vacuum. The transaction is designed to fit within a strategy. If the CDD team does not understand the context of this strategy, then it will be less well placed to do its job properly and to add value. Other points to agree on the terms of reference are scope, timing, responsibilities and reporting.

Prioritization is essential. CDD should focus on the areas of substantial uncertainty, risk and the potential upsides.

Three key questions

It is not practical for the terms of reference to address every last commercial issue facing the business. Prioritization is essential. CDD should focus on the areas of substantial uncertainty, risk and the potential upsides. Examples of each of these three key questions are set out below.

Uncertainty

- The market is set to accept this technology and take off, but will users commit now, having already hesitated for a number of years?
- The company to be acquired has a subsidiary in an unrelated business area, which the buyer would like to dispose of, but how it will fare and will it turn out to be an unattractive, unsaleable asset?

Risk

- The business is more profitable than all of its competitors, yet it has no structural reason to be so. How can one be sure that this is sustainable?
- Much of the success of the business depends on the successful launch of a new version of its key product. Will the product launch achieve what management claims?

Potential upsides

- The business is less profitable than its competitors and the acquirer wants to improve margins, but is this achievable?
- The US market is ripe for exploitation and it will just take a national distribution deal to achieve penetration. How realistic is that to achieve?

Therefore, in addition to a well-written brief it is useful to define the three key questions: the 'chairman' type questions focusing on the top strategic issues, such as those set out above.

Project kick-off meeting

The team should meet at the start of the commercial due diligence exercise to ensure that everyone has the clearest understanding of its objectives. At the kick-off meeting the full CDD team should:

- understand the strategic and operational context for the acquisition;
- agree its approach;
- share all of the information currently available in-house;
- prioritize areas of potential interest to the management team;
- discuss development options;
- decide responsibilities, contact points and reporting dates.

Of course, the team should stay in contact throughout the programme and liaise as information is gathered, when any problems are encountered or negatives arise.

Planning and desk research

The team now needs to prepare. It will already have internal papers relating to the transaction, such as a board paper or investment memorandum. It should have the sale memorandum from the investment bank or the target company's business plan.

The team should now access the wealth of publicly available information on the market and the target company. (Desk research sources are set out in the Appendix D.)

The team can start to define the major issues and plan how it will address them. It should also start to prepare for its meeting with management.

Meeting with management

It is now widely accepted that it is best practice to meet the management of the target company at the start of the CDD programme. When acquirers simply commissioned market research – as used to be the practice before commercial due diligence emerged as a discipline – such meetings were rare. The meeting with management of the target company at the outset of formal CDD serves the following purposes:

- reassuring the management that the CDD team is highly experienced in this work, appreciates the sensitivities involved and will not disrupt the business' current commercial relationships;
- 'selling' the benefits of the project to the management team: the value of the information to management, and the PR spin-off among customers;
- obtaining a thorough briefing on the business from the management itself;
- agreeing the best way for the CDD team to approach customers and other industry contacts;
- agreeing the set of internal contacts with whom the CDD team should be in touch;
- obtaining contact details of key customers and other managers who are familiar with the business;
- opening channels of communication so that important topics can be discussed or validated during the project.

The meeting with management can be delicate. It is best to use a team with extensive experience of these meetings, or at the very least of dealing with pressurized senior executives. Consultants should avoid the trap of alienating management by using business-school speak and failing to relate to the real world of management and its market. This is a very sensitive time for management; there is a lot at stake including the managers' livelihoods, and for owner-managers their retirement plans. The whole due diligence process can also be inherently stressful and disruptive. If the CDD team fails to build a positive relationship at this point, it will struggle to do its work effectively.

> **Consultants should avoid the trap of alienating management by using business-school speak and failing to relate to the real world of management and its market.**

Reassuring management and the vendor

Owner-managers tend to be very sensitive at the time of sale, simply because so much is at stake. Corporate vendors and private equity investors want to see a smooth process leading to a good result. When owners of businesses are thinking of selling, they rarely want to advertise the transaction. They fear that customers may suspend their orders until they know what will happen. Employees will become concerned and competitors will take as much advantage as they can. Even if the company is being acquired out of insolvency proceedings, management may need to be persuaded that a market investigation will lead to positive PR and not to more rumour and uncertainty.

> If commercial due diligence is to be carried out on an acquisition target, one of the first tasks of the people doing it will be to reassure the vendor and its representatives that they are responsible, discreet people who will not give the game away.

If commercial due diligence is to be carried out on an acquisition target, one of the first tasks for the people doing it will be to reassure the vendor and its representatives that they are responsible, discreet people who will not give the game away. They need to demonstrate a good understanding of the sensitivities surrounding a transaction, and should be able to point to a solid track record of successful projects in the past.

Wise vendors appreciate that a thorough commercial due diligence exercise is beneficial to them. Two key reasons are:

- It demonstrates that the buyer is a professional organization, which provides comfort if the vendor is to have any continuing link with the business it is selling. Even when the vendor is a large group which is divesting all interest in the target company, it will often feel a duty of care towards its soon-to-be former employees.

- The review provides invaluable market understanding for the management of the target business after the acquisition process is complete. It is not simply a document to be thrown away once the deal is done.

Selling the benefits

The management team could have done without the CDD team turning up at an already busy time and asking detailed questions. To break down barriers, it is a good idea for the CDD team to point out the possible benefits of the process to management. A useful approach is to ask managers what issues they would like the commercial due diligence programme to address. This works because it:

• helps to build the relationship;

• can identify areas of concern to the management, which they may not have discussed with the buyer;

• can add value to the whole exercise.

Briefing on the business

What better place to get a briefing on the business than from management? In less then half a day management can give the CDD team a full view of the company and its market. This sends the CDD team rapidly up the learning curve and allows it to save a lot of time.

It is important to get managers to relax and to stop them overselling the business. If they do oversell, it will be discovered later. The aim is to have a full and frank discussion about the business, its opportunities and the challenges it faces.

Through its meeting with management the commercial team has the opportunity to form a view of the management team as a whole and of the key individuals. In particular, the commercial team can comment on management's ability to assess its markets and the competitive position of the business. It is always worth asking the commercial team its opinion on these topics.

Basis for market interviews – disclosure and confidentiality

One of the best platforms for speaking to customers is a customer-care survey commissioned by the target company. This, of course, requires the full co-operation of the target's management and it must fit in with the company's customer relationship programme.

A key parameter of the CDD project to establish with management is whether the customer interviews are disclosed or not. The CDD team needs to talk to people in the market and it needs to explain the reason for the work to interviewees without compromising confidentiality. This requires a 'platform' for making enquiries. One of the best platforms for speaking to customers is a customer-care survey commissioned by the target company. This, of course, requires the full co-operation of the target's management and it must fit in with the company's customer relationship programme. Naturally, management must be reassured that its sensitivities are fully understood and that customer relationships will be respected. Management may offer to hand over existing customer surveys. In reality, very few companies conduct customer-care surveys which approach the level of professionalism and detail which a well run CDD programme involves, so prior surveys are almost inevitably of little practical use.

> **In reality, very few companies conduct customer-care surveys which approach the level of professionalism and detail which a well run CDD programme involves, so prior surveys are almost inevitably of little practical use.**

Contacting competitors is obviously not normally possible using the customer-care approach. Thus, there is no need to discuss the topic in detail with management. The CDD team can make its own enquiries in this arena, so long as it does not compromise confidentiality.

The vendor, or its financial adviser running the transaction, can influence the process and attempt to limit the number of discussions which are held. Of course, it is absolutely reasonable for a vendor to wish to protect confidentiality and to understand the nature of the discussions. Indeed, it is in the acquirer's own interest to avoid unhelpful rumours in the market which could destabilize relationships between the company and its customers. What is not reasonable is for the vendor to seek to prevent the acquirer from talking on a confidential or undisclosed basis to the people who know the real strengths and weaknesses of the company. The seller who seeks to prevent reasonable access to important sources of information, such as customers, runs the risk of appearing to hide unpleasant facts, which is usually counterproductive.

Agreeing internal contacts

To avoid any breach of confidentiality the CDD team needs to know who in the management team is aware of the transaction. The CDD team may also want to interview some key managers. Although the focus of CDD is primarily external, a small number of key internal contacts should help to clarify the commercial position of the business. Only a few managers need to be interviewed, for example, it makes sense to interview managing directors of subsidiaries and senior customer-facing managers in the initial project phase of internal meetings.

If customers are to be interviewed on behalf of the target company, you must ensure that customer-facing staff are aware of the research programme. Otherwise, there can be embarrassment and confusion when the target company's sales director is surprised to hear a key customer mention a discussion he has just had with an unknown representative of the company.

Selection of interview targets

The selection of customers for interview is a delicate process. The CDD team to some extent is reliant on management to provide good contacts and good information as to which contacts are relevant. Some management teams are tempted to hand pick reference customers and to sweep any problem cases under the carpet. It is, of course, possible to see through this by reviewing customer lists from the sales system or from debtor lists, but it is best to avoid using this approach in the first place.

Management may be wary of some of the other contacts which the CDD team will want to take up. There may be sensitivity over suppliers if contracts are currently being negotiated. Former employees can be a particularly sensitive area. They are often considered to be poor sources as they have been mentally ostracized – part of a natural management defence mechanism. The trick is to see through this and assess those cases where there is good information to be gained.

Ideally, the entire interview programme, including interviews with competitors, should be agreed with management.

Ideally, the entire interview programme, including interviews with competitors, should be agreed with management. However, the CDD team should not accept being spoon-fed and it should make its own decisions about whom to contact while ensuring that it does not conduct any interviews which disrupt the business.

Building a relationship and opening channels of communication

Once a good relationship has been established with management, business issues can be discussed in an open manner. If trust has not been established, management will tend either to be sceptical and reserved or remain in 'sales mode' providing only a PR view of the business. In one example AMR worked on, we established that a technical ceramics company which had led the market for many years faced the prospect of its two leading competitors launching highly innovative products at the forthcoming key International trade show. Presented with this information, the managing director admitted that he had mishandled product development and that his company was about to fall behind for the first time in its history. This admission was fundamental to the value of the business.

Final preparation

After the meeting with management, the team can review its planning and finalize its preparation by:

- ensuring that it has a clear understanding of the key commercial issues;
- determining which analytical tools and methods it intends to use;
- starting to analyse the key issues;
- preparing its question sets for the interviews and making minor revisions as necessary;
- developing a research programme including the final targeting of organizations for interview.

Information gathering 5

There are three sources of information in a commercial due diligence programme:

1 external published information (also known as secondary);
2 external unpublished information (also known as primary);
3 internal information.

Secondary sources

The detailed research phase starts with a desk-research exercise, reviewing all relevant published sources (see Appendix D for suggestions). A substantial volume of information is easily available from public sources and through commercial databases. Consultancies conducting CDD may also already have relevant data on the target markets.

> **The desk research continues throughout the project. As the issues develop, the desk research becomes increasingly focused.**

The desk research continues throughout the project. As the issues develop, the desk research becomes increasingly focused. With so much information available through public sources, desk researchers run the risk of happening across useful information, but possibly not the best. Using inferior information obviously reduces the quality of the subsequent analysis. Instead of just going online, you should develop a desk-research strategy.

Some basic tenets on designing desk research strategies are:

- Know what you need to be looking for and why you need it. How does it fit with the bigger picture? How are you going to use it when you get it?
- Integrate desk research with the overall research design.
- Know what sources are available and develop a checklist of information sources to use.
- Develop keywords to assist in online searches.

There are three main desk-research resources:

1 external library resources;
2 online databases;
3 the Internet.

Library resources

The main business research libraries in London are the business reference room at the British Library (St Pancras), the City Business Library, and the DTI Export Library.

Broadly, London's business libraries can be categorized as follows:

British Library. Best overall coverage, including an excellent range of online databases.

City Business Library Most helpful staff and user-friendly environment. Good coverage of materials: e.g. market research reports/business directories. Useful to check on coverage of a particular subject prior to visiting – ring in advance. Staff may also provide advice on additional research sources.

DTI Export Library Good on international market and company information, including international company directories.

Of course, there are extensive library resources in other major cities throughout the world.

Specialist libraries

Professional associations, trade associations and industry bodies often have libraries which are open to the general public. You usually have to make an appointment and sometimes there is a nominal fee. It is certainly worth establishing whether the industry body has a library. This information is often available from its website or can be found by a quick phone call. It is also worth consulting the *Listing of Specialist Libraries* held in the British Library (shelfmark: BS10/489). Similar resources are available at libraries in other major cities.

Online databases

Coverage of online databases falls into three main categories, detailed below.

Business news

These collate business news items from a wide range of publications. Similar products are provided by a number of vendors. Reuters Business Briefing is an excellent business news database. Alternative services include Lexis-Nexis and Newswire. The easiest way to access these information sources is through subscription. Given the high level of competition between the rival sources, terms are often negotiable. These sources can also be accessed from external libraries. In the UK – Lexis-Nexis at the British Library and Newswire at the British Library and the City Business Library.

Company financials

Coverage falls into two main categories: global coverage of quoted companies (e.g. Investext, FT Sequencer); and national coverage of a broader range of companies (e.g. UK: Companies House Direct, FAME, France: ORT). AMADEUS includes company financial data for the whole of the European Union. In the UK, it is available at the British Library. The breadth and depth of coverage within national-level databases is determined by the legislation on company reporting in force in each country.

Market data

Sector/consumer information is contained in databases such as the World Marketing forecast, which is available at the British Library. Detail on markets in individual countries is available from sources such as EIU and World markets online. These databases are available at selected business libraries.

Specialist online databases

There is a specialist database for just about every subject. There is, however, no single, independently operated directory of online databases, although Dialog/Datastar provides a comprehensive listing of its databases at the following address:

ds.datastarweb.com/ds/products/datastar/ds.htm

A summary of the main online databases is provided in Table 5.1.

Table 5.1 Summary of coverage and location of key online databases

Database	Company financials				Business news				Market			Country-specific information		
	UK	France	Germany	EU	Global (quoted)	UK	France	Germany	EU	Global	Sector information	Consumer characteristics	National characteristics	Company data
Reuters Business Briefing				Y*	Y*					Y	Y*			
Companies House Direct	Y													
FAME	Y										Y*			
ORT		Y												
GENIOS			Y					Y				Y		
Creditreform Germany			Y	Y										
FIZ								Y						
AMADEUS				Y							Y*			
EIU Business Intelligence													Y	
Infotrac (Investext)						Y					Y			
Lexis-Nexis						Y				Y				
World marketing forecasts											Y	Y	Y	
MAPS											Y			

* Limited coverage
† Free access to partial service

The Internet

You should note that material held in separate searchable databases will not be listed on search engines, so searching often needs to be a two-stage process: (1) identify the separate searchable databases and (2) search them. This also holds implications for the search terms used: the question as ever is 'What are we actually looking for?'. It is often useful to try a more generic search to find the directories and lists.

Appendix D lists useful information sources and websites in greater detail.

Desk-research limitations

Secondary sources have their limitations. First, they are general rather than specific: large, mass markets are often covered in considerable detail, whereas small, niche markets are referred to in passing. Second, they are rarely completely up to date: in business, as soon as information appears in print it is out of date. As the pace of competition increases, yesterday's news is today's ancient history.

Paradoxically, the electronic revolution both mitigates and aggravates these shortfalls of secondary sources. Commercial databases and the Internet contain more information than whole libraries did ten years ago, and because the cost of updating and republishing information has slumped, they can be far more up to date.

But the greater availability of information is one of the drivers accelerating the pace of competition. Ten years ago executives may have had to rely on information that was a year old, but that was not a problem because things had probably not changed too much in the interim. Now we can have last month's information, but in the meantime key aspects of the industry may be changing.

Secondary sources are invaluable as a precursor to investigations in the market, using primary sources. They provide basic data and they can give the commercial due diligence team valuable background information about the industry – its history, its folklore and its terminology. Talking to people in an industry is far easier if the industry participants think they are dealing with someone who understands the basic issues they deal with from day to day – if they have to explain the basics, they will get bored and lose patience.

Primary sources

A key part of a commercial due diligence programme is the series of detailed discussions with customers, distributors, regulators, competitors, industry observers, and other relevant contacts in the market. Even in very well documented industries such as telecoms and financial services these interviews remain essential. The industry's reputable published, statistical reports should be exploited to the full. But it is not possible to segment the market or analyse key purchase criteria without speaking to market participants.

Figure 5.1 shows a generic list of the various primary information sources which a CDD team typically considers calling on.

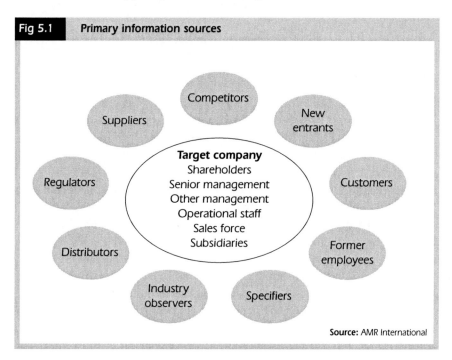

Fig 5.1 Primary information sources

Source: AMR International

Customers

It is very rare to undertake a commercial due diligence exercise without speaking to at least a number of customers. Customers are best grouped into three categories:

1 current;
2 former;
3 non/lost prospects or failed tenders/proposals.

No other group's opinions are as important as the customers'. If customers hold a business in high esteem and will continue to buy from it, then its future is likely to be healthy; if customers' purchasing or loyalty is declining, then the future looks bleak.

Case study – Ferranti

In 1988 Ferranti bought International Signal Controls (ISC). Ferranti was a long-established British electronics company with particular expertise in the defence sector. ISC was an American defence electronics company which claimed to have won a series of lucrative contracts with the defence procurement bodies of a range of foreign governments.

It took some time for the fact to be discovered that several of these contracts did not exist, and it was two years before the resultant gaping hole in Ferranti's balance sheet finally sank the company. Parts of the company survive within former competitors like Marconi and Thales.

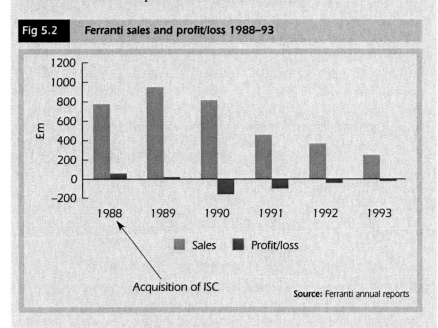

Fig 5.2   **Ferranti sales and profit/loss 1988–93**

Acquisition of ISC

Source: Ferranti annual reports

One reason why Ferranti bought ISC was to defend itself against a likely hostile bid from another British group, STC. Ferranti knew that STC had looked at ISC itself but had decided against going ahead. Ferranti believed that acquiring ISC would create a sort of poison pill, and thus divert STC's attention. It did, but the pill was more poisonous than expected.

ISC persuaded Ferranti that certain contracts were too sensitive to be investigated, and that following the acquisition they would need to be 'ring-fenced' and run separately from the main business. Ferranti, in a hurry to close the deal before STC's bid materialized, agreed.

33

Amazingly, none of the claimed customers was approached to confirm the existence of the contracts. Admittedly, the nature of the business made such contacts more difficult than is usually the case – and one of the most important contacts had the misfortune to make an unplanned exit from a helicopter in mid-flight. But these obstacles do not diminish the need for proper commercial due diligence. The financial due diligence was also limited – as Ferranti relied on the audit – but it was the failure to carry out commercial due diligence that sank the ship.

Lessons learned: however large, important or complex the deal, acquirers should not lose sight of customers. Customer interviews are at the heart of CDD and are an essential part of the acquisition process.

Distributors

Many businesses do not have contact with their final customers. This makes distributors, wholesalers, resellers, retailers or whoever else sells the product on almost as important as the end customers themselves. These distributors are the company's direct customers and they are almost inevitably better informed than the end users about the detailed workings of the target company and the strengths and weaknesses of its products. It is the job of distributors to understand their customers, so it should be possible to obtain a clear view of the market's current and future needs from them.

Example

Sometimes the relationship between principal and distributor is not straightforward. For example, a leading French financial services company once sold half its products through one nationally organized distributor, the post office. But enquiries revealed that this distributor strongly objected to certain conditions of its seven-year contract with the principal. These conditions had been acceptable at the start of the contract period, but had been rendered obsolete by changes in the industry. The principal obstinately refused to amend the terms of the contract, and the distributor was actively planning to stop dealing with that principal once the contract came to an end, which was in less than one year's time. This would have wiped out half of the principal's sales.

Specifiers

Specifiers can be as influential as customers and distributors in certain businesses, most notably in the construction industry. Although architects and surveyors have seen their power wane as design-and-build permeates the top end of the industry, their importance as specifiers of many building products should not be underestimated. If the architect has specified a product 'or equivalent' then there is a strong chance that the builder will choose to use it.

The role of specifier extends beyond construction. Doctors are often specifiers of pharmaceuticals and care homes. IT consultants may be specifiers of computer hardware and software. Teachers are the specifiers of school books.

Regulators

Governments and quangos can have a profound impact on industries – often in ways which are quite unforeseen. When the UK government started to encourage employees to make personal arrangements for their pensions it did not foresee the possibility that the pensions industry would adopt the kind of forcible selling techniques which have given the sector a bad name. This mistake has caused untold anxiety as well as an enormous waste of money and energy in unravelling the mis-sold policies.

The future plans of regulators are not a factor of all commercial due diligence reviews, but they can be critical. Consider the following three scenarios.

Example 1

The target company was launching an alternative directory enquiries service in various French countries. Deregulation of directory enquiries services across Europe may well be opening up opportunities for new service providers, but slow implementation and the ability of incumbents to slow liberalization can delay the development of new entrants. In such cases, new entrants' substantial set-up costs are recouped more slowly and their well-worked business plans are rendered invalid.

Example 2

The target company manufactured a particular kind of safe. The UK regulations require this kind of safe to withstand attack by a thermal lance for a period of 15 seconds. The equivalent German regulations require it to withstand a force comparable to that of a tank! As with many industries, the European Commission had the unenviable task of 'harmonizing' these very different requirements, and it was important to ascertain the likely direction of future legislation. By talking to the relevant EC Directorate as well as numerous well-informed industry sources, we were able to satisfy ourselves that the more rigorous German standards would not be imposed across the board.

Example 3

The target company made spare parts for lorries. The parts were 'generic', in that they met the same technical and performance specifications as the original parts, but they were not made or badged by the OEM, the original equipment maker. An important part of the rationale for the deal was the possibility of exporting the company's products to other European countries, and this meant understanding the current and likely future attitude of continental European regulators towards such 'copy' parts for vehicles.

Suppliers

Suppliers can be an excellent source of information in a commercial due diligence programme. If you want to buy a Ford dealership, it would be a good idea to find out what Ford thinks of the business and its prospects. If you are buying a cable maker – or any other capital intensive manufacturer – then it is worth interviewing the major equipment suppliers. They should know their target customers well. They can comment on or even benchmark the level of capital expenditure or manufacturing efficiency of the target company against its competitors. Suppliers are normally hungry for more information on their target markets and are keen to identify new angles into customers. This makes them willing to talk to outsiders.

Competitors

Competitors usually keep a close eye on each other. They serve the same customers – or at least the same type of customers. In addition, they recruit from the same labour pool, and in many industries they recruit from each other.

Acquirers should consider the importance of obtaining competitor information and the type of approach which would be needed before deciding how to carry out their commercial due diligence.

Competitors often have the most carefully researched information about the state of the market and its future prospects. They will also have searched out and studied the weaknesses of the target company, and will usually be happy to explain them to anyone who listens. An ideal question to ask a competitor might be: 'So, given your comments, if you were running xyz (target company) what would you do?'.

It is hard for in-house commercial due diligence teams to interview competitors as they have the wrong calling card. Consultancies vary in their attitudes to competitor interviews. Some will not approach competitors at all; others will use so-called 'pretext enquiries' to gain access. Obviously, they must not use unacceptable or illegal practices. Acquirers should consider the importance of obtaining competitor information and the type of approach which would be needed before deciding how to carry out their commercial due diligence.

Former employees

Former employees can be an excellent source of information, but they are not always easy to include in the research programme. First, they can be hard to find. Then, once found, their opinions sometimes have to be discounted as they can have personal reasons for liking or disliking their former employer and their former colleagues, particularly if they left under difficult circumstances.

In cases where access to the target company is not available, the importance of former employees rises. In a covert commercial due diligence exercise, if you can find a former employee who is prepared to discuss his former employer while remaining dispassionate, he can turn out to be the single most valuable external source of information.

> **Example**
>
> In an investigation of a market-leading instrumentation company, the customers unanimously agreed that the company had the best products in its market, thanks to a first-class R&D department. The commercial team spoke to some R&D people employed by the main competitor, only to discover that they were recent recruits from the target company. It transpired that the target company's management had downsized the R&D department in order to improve the results of a disappointing year. The move was effective in the short term, but in the long term the company would clearly suffer from a lack of new products in an increasingly competitive market.

New entrants to a market will usually carry out a considerable amount of independent research before taking a market entry decision, so their views are normally worth listening to.

New entrants

Perhaps the hardest type of contact to identify is the company planning to enter a market. But sometimes companies will advertise their intention to enter a market well in advance, and then they are typically willing to speak with outsiders in order to enhance their own understanding of what they are getting into. In technical markets the research community will often get wind of potential developments. Networking helps to identify new entrants and can provide a good basis for conversations.

New entrants to a market will usually carry out a considerable amount of independent research before taking a market entry decision, so their views are normally worth listening to.

Industry observers

Industry observers include trade journalists, trade association officials, academics, and consultants. These people follow developments in their industries closely, and are familiar with many of the major players. Talking to them should provide a good introductory briefing to an industry or to the key issues within the industry. Industry observers can also refer you to other useful contacts. The downside is that industry observers have their own agendas, and it is just as well to be aware of them.

Consultants are keen to avoid giving away their hard-won expertise without payment, and sometimes it is worthwhile entering into a commercial arrangement with them. However, even consultants are often willing to have a brief conversation without payment, as it helps them to keep up to date in their own field.

Trade journalists are keen to be the first to break any new story, and it is important to be particularly circumspect with them. They are often extremely good at detecting that something more is going on than meets the eye. Having

Generally, the more niche the industry, the more accessible and talkative the trade journalists.

said that, trade journalists are often talkative. They have built up considerable expertise and are rarely contacted by people from outside their industry or by people whose main aim is not simply to plant a story promoting some product or service. Generally, the more niche the industry, the more accessible and talkative the trade journalists.

Example

A quoted group planned to enter the German portakabin market through acquisition. It was negotiating with a potential target and had others in its sights. However, its market information was limited and there was apparently little publicly available information on the market.

Through a series of telephone calls and contacts made at a regional construction industry trade show, the commercial team identified an industry expert based in the Ruhrgebeit. This journalist published an annual review of the portakabin market as a supplement to a construction journal. The commercial team met with this expert and both sides compared notes. The expert pointed to some vital information, including the quality of various companies' fleets, and their sales and distribution methods.

These insights allowed the commercial team to focus their enquiries on the key issues in the German market and to benchmark the target company. This exposed its weaknesses in key performance areas, relative to the competition. The proposed acquisition was abandoned and an alternative market-entry route was sought.

Academics are often primarily interested in furthering their research, and small parcels of information which are not backed up by surveys based on rigorous statistical sampling methods may be of minor interest to them. They are rarely useful sources in a commercial due diligence enquiry, although they may be of help in understanding technical aspects of a product or service.

At the other end of the spectrum is a complicated transaction which requires holding face-to-face discussions with large numbers of very senior people in a highly researched industry (e.g. computers) or in a secretive industry (e.g. pharmaceuticals) and in different countries.

Trade associations are mostly helpful in providing lists of further contacts. They have to be extremely careful to avoid being seen to promote the interests of one member above the others, so they are rarely willing to offer opinions about individual companies. Nonetheless, they can often help to describe some of the key characteristics of the industry, which helps to inform later discussions.

How many discussions?

A significant variable to the scope and cost of a commercial due diligence programme is the number of discussions which need to be held, the type of people to be contacted, and the way they are interviewed.

On a small transaction in a rarely researched and unsecretive industry, contacting a small number of middle-level executives by telephone can quickly cover a lot of ground. At the other end of the spectrum is a complicated transaction which requires holding face-to-face discussions with large numbers of very senior people in a highly researched industry (e.g. computers) or in a secretive industry (e.g. pharmaceuticals) and in different countries.

The number of people to be contacted is determined by the:

- number of markets;
- number of countries;
- level of uncertainty;
- level of risk;
- quality of published data.

It may be that the target operates in many markets and many countries, but that most of these areas are well documented and well understood. The initial issue analysis should have identified those sectors or territories which are either critical to the future performance of the whole business, or which are producing troubling results and require detailed investigation and analysis. As we have noted before, the typical time frame of a commercial due diligence project may not permit an exhaustive study of every aspect of a large business.

The personal approach

Personal meetings usually generate more information and insights than telephone discussions. Most people are more relaxed during face-to-face conversations than during phone conversations – we are all reassured when we can see the face of the person we are speaking to and can gauge the reaction we are provoking. When people are relaxed they become more expansive and more discursive. It is far harder to give one-word answers face to face than over the phone. In a meeting you can share papers or even fill in a chart together.

People are not only more relaxed when then can see each others' faces; they communicate better. Psychological researchers have shown that only a small fraction of what we communicate is transmitted by voice: the rest is transmitted by body language – especially by facial expression. Thus a face-to-face business discussion will usually generate more useful information than a telephone conversation.

Psychological researchers have shown that only a small fraction of what we communicate is transmitted by voice; the rest is transmitted by body language – especially by facial expression. Thus a face-to-face business discussion will usually generate more useful information than a telephone conversation.

On the other hand, personal meetings take up far more time. Not just the time spent travelling, and waiting in office receptions, but also the time spent arranging the meeting in the first place. Arranging a meeting with, say, a marketing director of a drug company can take as much time as actually holding a detailed phone conversation with a less junior manager or less pressured person in an industry less concerned about confidentiality.

The answer in most cases is to carry out a mixture of face-to-face meetings and telephone discussions. The best ratio will vary from case to case, according to how secretive the industry is and how critical is the information held by particular individuals. A ratio of one meeting to 10 phone calls is not uncommon.

Why do people agree to talk?

This is probably the question most commonly asked about commercial due diligence information gathering. Managers outside the target company are not being paid for their participation in the project, and they are not likely to win a new customer for their business, so why do they talk?

- The flippant reason is that the people who carry out commercial due diligence have to be pleasant, persuasive people to talk to which means that the respondents are charmed into submission.

- The cynical reason is that when busy people with interesting jobs talk about their jobs, in effect, they are being encouraged to talk about themselves.

- The psychological reason is that when people explain a process or a situation to intelligent, encouraging listeners, they are forced to get their own thoughts on the subject in order. They re-evaluate their notions as they go along, and may come up with some interesting new ways of looking at things. You may find yourself enjoying a conversation in which you are doing most of the talking, not because you are a rampant egomaniac, but because you are reviewing your own ideas as you go along – a valuable process.

> **The surprising reason why people talk to consultants is they get something in return.**

- The surprising reason why people talk to consultants is they get something in return. Experienced consultants are practised at analysing an industry or a sector in a short space of time. A desk-research exercise combined with introductory briefings from the client and some friendly contacts will often enable a good consultant to make some observations which even the most experienced (and most cynical) market participant will find valuable. Good commercial due diligence interviews are a two-way street, not simply a process of sucking information from unwitting victims.

Getting the most from semi-structured discussions

A great deal of planning and a great deal of expertise goes into the preparation for the discussions in a commercial due diligence project. Each discussion is a demanding exercise, because the people leading the discussions need to achieve three things simultaneously. They must:

1 provide sufficient interest to maintain the attention of the person being interviewed. This means being polite (perhaps even charming), but more importantly it means asking intelligent, stimulating questions, and occasionally providing interesting information or ideas in return.

2 keep the discussion directed towards the areas of interest – and this process of direction must appear neither clumsy nor manipulative.

3 constantly evaluate the information being received, and assess it in the context of the information already possessed. The direction of the conversation may be radically affected by what is said during it.

The person gathering the information may script in advance an introductory paragraph, crafting it carefully to maximize its appeal to the specific person being contacted. Thereafter he or she will probably rely on a checklist of the issues to be covered, although certain questions may be drafted in detail and rehearsed.

The questions should be ordered so that the person contacted is not intimidated or alienated. For instance, the size of the market may be the logical place to start an analysis of a market, but it could be a crass first question to a minor market participant who is more concerned with about individual customers and products or services, and who is unlikely to have a good estimate of the total market size on the tip of his/her tongue. It is usually better to start the conversation around the contact's own business or experience, steering away from potentially sensitive areas until a rapport has been built up.

Do people tell the truth?

As if doing a commercial due diligence exercise is not difficult enough already, the people contacted during the exercise can sometimes mislead. They rarely tell straightforward lies, but they often fail to tell the truth. For instance, they can:

- fail to remember or misremember certain important facts;
- misinterpret or misunderstand the question and provide the right answer to another question – for example, giving the market size for all apples as opposed to green apples;
- be ignorant of the detail in the first place, but concerned about appearing less knowledgeable than they think they should be and so they provide a well-intentioned, but misleading answer;
- withhold information because they are uncertain how it will be used.

Good commercial due diligence practitioners are people who can quickly build positive relationships with other people – but who remain sceptical. Experienced interviewers think on their feet. They can spot erroneous or incoherent information

> **It is essential to obtain corroboration of any important findings from a number of sources. The more important the finding is in the context of the overall project, the more corroboration is required.**

and then find a sympathetic way in which to challenge it. Even with these skills, it is essential to obtain corroboration of any important findings from a number of sources. The more important the finding is in the context of the overall project, the more corroboration is required.

From time to time a business comes up for sale because the vendor can foresee serious problems ahead. Perhaps it knows that the market has peaked and is about to turn down, or it has heard plans of a market entry by a major new competitor. This sort of thing is more often encountered with a private vendor than a corporate one. Experienced and sceptical commercial due diligence team members will always try to read between the lines and keep asking themselves 'Why is this business being sold?'.

Internal information

Commercial due diligence should not rely solely on information provided by the company or internal information. Nonetheless, internal information is required to understand the business and allow external comparisons. The commercial due diligence team will normally request the business plan, performance measures and market-related information.

Business plan

The business plan is the key document. It is the job of the commercial due diligence team to validate its projections and the assumptions that lie behind it. In a MBO, management will have prepared the plan. In a corporate acquisition the acquirer may rely on management's forecasts or strategic plan. Alternatively, the forecasts may have been reworked and represented by the seller's corporate finance house, in an *information memorandum* (IM). An IM is a sales document, which inevitably presents the business in the best possible light: watch out for unsubstantiated claims, 3D graphics and graphs which do not begin at zero.

The business plan may go through a number of versions and will be verified by the financial due diligence team. It is essential to get everyone to use the same version of the plan.

Performance measures

Management should be able to provide performance measures on the business. Key performance indicators (KPIs) are hard measures, although not typically based on financial information.

Examples of KPIs include:

- hotel occupancy rates;
- production 'up time';
- product reject rate;
- consultant loading rates;
- sales conversion ratios;
- advertising page yield;
- completed visits per service engineer.

Whilst an internal analysis of the KPIs across a division or from one year to another is useful, the real value comes from competitor benchmarking. This requires careful planning and advanced interview skills to ensure that the information obtained from competitors can be used for valid comparisons.

Market-related information

The commercial due diligence team should come away from the initial meeting with the management of the target company armed with all the relevant market information the company holds. Reports and documents to ask for include:

- market reports;
- customer surveys;
- customer lists;
- development papers;
- trade magazines;
- trade show catalogues.

Obtaining this information from management saves valuable time in a commercial due diligence exercise. However, it can be tempting for the team to rely too heavily on the information provided by management. If key data are not corroborated from external sources, the results of the commercial due diligence programme can be compromised. For example, management may report that the market is worth $1 bn but this figure should only be used once properly verified. It is rarely the case that management has quantified and segmented the market accurately. If the company has sales of $50 m and the market is supposedly worth $1 bn you can be fairly sure that its addressable segment will be much less than the $1 bn figure taken from a market report.

It is rarely the case that management has quantified and segmented the market accurately.

45

The outputs of commercial due diligence 6

The reporting process

The outputs of a commercial due diligence exercise centre around the final report. It is best not to go for a 'big bang' style of presentation and then walk away. The ground should be prepared carefully, particularly if there is bad or surprising news.

Feedback and reporting on a major CDD exercise with a three- to four-week timetable are typically handled as follows:

- feedback during the process at fixed points or as key points emerge;
- draft report 48 hours before the presentation;
- presentation of the draft final report;
- submission of the final report 48 hours after the presentation.

The feedback during the process need not always be formal. When significant issues arise which could affect the transaction, they should be fed back rapidly and their consequences integrated into the process. In extreme cases these issues can stop the transaction. In other cases they become the focus of attention and other advisers can be asked to focus and report on them as appropriate.

It makes sense to circulate drafts of the final report to all those who will attend the final presentation. This allows them to digest the information and ask better questions at the presentation. It also forces the CDD provider to be prepared in advance! Of course, these drafts

> **The final copy of the report should be circulated 48 hours after the presentation.**

will be replaced by the final reports. The final copy of the report should be circulated 48 hours after the presentation. This will then be the definitive document.

In an ideal world, the CDD team would provide interim reports or attend an interim presentation. In reality, this good discipline is hard to maintain. If the process is not well controlled, the CDD team can end up spending more time participating in conference calls and on reporting than on doing its work.

The presentation

The presentation of findings is very valuable because the commercial due diligence is only one of a number of inputs to the decision-making process. The acquirer's acquisition team will listen to the commercial due diligence presentation in the context of what it has already learned from its own discussions and from other presentations. The acquirers will then wish to ask questions of the commercial due diligence team, focusing on those issues which have the greatest impact on the transaction. This question-and-answer process ensures that the findings of the commercial due diligence are fully understood, and further develops the findings by comparing and contrasting them with the findings from other sources.

It can be useful to have present at this session the advisers handling other elements of the transaction. As long as petty rivalries do not flare up, this helps to ensure that the maximum firepower is focused on answering the key questions.

In highly time-pressured private equity transactions, the investor can be tempted to invite all parties to the presentation (excluding the seller, of course). This can be a mistake. The investor or acquirer is seeking the clearest possible view of the business and its prospects. Management no doubt has a clear view, but it is its own; if overeager managers attend the presentation, they can end up disrupting the proceedings by pushing their own case, resulting in diversions up various garden paths and away from the defining issues. If the lending banks are to be invited, the investor must be confident that any bad news or factors which could damage cash flow have already been identified. If some negatives are overdramatized, then the banks can take fright and be put off the transaction.

Obviously the vendor should not be privy to the report, at least in the first instance. However, as a part of the negotiations, the buyer may choose to release part or even all of the report to the vendor as a tactic to prove that the business has less value than originally thought.

Obviously the vendor should not be privy to the report, at least in the first instance. However, as a part of the negotiations, the buyer may choose to release part or even all of the report to the vendor as a tactic to prove that the business has less value than originally thought.

The report

The presentation is often the highlight of the commercial due diligence process. Nonetheless, the report has to be clear, well written and self-explanatory, with footnotes and cross references if need be.

In the case of a private equity investment, the audience for the written report will include:

- the private equity investor;
- syndicated investors;
- other advisers working on the transaction;
- lending banks;
- management.

Each one of these groups will inevitably have different concerns and will be looking for different information from the report.

- Private equity investors want a clear view of whether they are about to make a good investment, and the extent of the key risks.
- Syndicated investors are looking for comfort on the quality of the investment. They are inevitably less close to the transaction than the lead investor.
- The other advisers involved in the valuation will be looking for forecast analyses on which they can base their valuations.
- Lending banks will focus on areas of potential risk to cash flow. These will influence the terms on which they will provide debt.
- Management will be concerned if the report does not provide an accurate representation of the company and its market. Depending on the future role of management, and any possible difference between the valuation and either an upside or a downside case, managers may be more, or less, vociferous. Management will also be most interested to see the post-transaction recommendations.

A lot hangs on the report. Many of its readers may not have attended the presentation, and will not have benefited from the subsequent question and answer sessions during which key issues are fleshed out.

There is no standard report format or template. The reporting topics and style differ according to the transaction, who is doing the work and, most importantly, the audience. Table 6.1 shows the format of a typical report. It is certainly not the only way to present the output of a commercial due diligence exercise, but it is a format which has stood the test of time and has proved highly satisfactory for a wide variety of acquirers and investors.

Table 6.1	A commercial due diligence report template
Report section	*Explanation*
Contents	
Terms of reference	The brief and the methodology used to fulfil it.
The answer on a page	A single page of bullet points, summarizing all of the key issues.
Conclusions	Key conclusions for each of the individual markets, business units and revenue streams analysed.
Analysis	Structured analysis of all of the key issues which have culminated in the conclusions.
	The analysis should be based on factual information. When facts are not available, opinions should be used, as long as they can be substantiated.
Contact reports and profiles	Records of all important discussions, and profiles of key players in the market.
Appendices	Background explanatory material about the company and its industry.
Executive summary (optional)	A formal written explanation of the 'answer' and conclusions.

Towards a recommendation

The whole work programme should be driving towards a clear recommendation. It is important for the people carrying out the commercial due diligence to bear this in mind at all times. The key is to be able to answer 'the chairman's question', namely, 'Is it a good idea to buy this company?'. There can only be three answers:

- Yes
- No
- Yes, if you can satisfy yourselves that problems or threats identified can be mitigated, or if you can negotiate the terms of the deal to cater for them.

The prospective acquirer should certainly insist that the commercial due diligence team gives one of these answers at the end of their presentation. Some advisers are expert at caveating their answers. Acquirers and investors do not like these caveats, because by the time they have navigated their way through the weasel words, they hardly know where they stand. Whilst the CDD team certainly should have a clear view of the market and the company's competitive position, it can reasonably caveat its recommendation if there are elements to the acquisition decision – such as valuation multiples – which the CDD team is ill-equipped to comment on. Nonetheless, it should be in the business of providing a clear answer.

> **Whilst the CDD team certainly should have a clear view of the market and the company's competitive position, it can reasonably caveat its recommendation if there are elements to the acquisition decision – such as valuation multiples – which the CDD team is ill-equipped to comment on.**

Reporting topics

Beyond the 'answer', the wish-list of information about a company you are about to buy is never ending. However, an inevitable aspect of acquiring a company is that the time available for investigation and negotiation is severely limited. The vendor does not want its management to be tied up in endless meetings answering questions about the business which have no beneficial impact on the way it is run from day to day. Equally, they do not want current or potential competitors to make prolonged investigations into all the important relationships the company has. Vendors want to minimize the extent to which a due diligence programme destabilizes the business.

Commercial due diligence exercises are allowed no more than four or five weeks – and often less. Because time is short, it is essential to focus on the critical issues. The commercial due diligence should concentrate its efforts on the areas of least information and greatest risk.

Most acquirers will have a reasonable amount of information about their targets before they start negotiating (perhaps from the preliminary investigation described above). There will be other areas where information is not available and is hard to obtain, or areas of the business which merit futher investigation. For example, some product lines or country markets may be new or unfamiliar; questions may be raised about key managers, business processes, lead-generation, customer services, or reputation for innovation. For instance, there may be

It would be rare for a commercial due diligence programme to be able to review every aspect of this checklist, in detail, but parts of it will figure in the 'deliverables' section of any work programme or proposal.

particular product lines which are unfamiliar to the acquirer. This information should be requested and gathered, but the key is to analyse the critical issues and bring this together into a coherent view of the business.

A fairly comprehensive list of issues and, therefore, reporting topics, is given in the checklist below. It would be rare for a commercial due diligence programme to be able to review every aspect of this checklist in detail, but parts of it will figure in the 'deliverables' section of any work programme or proposal.

Commercial due diligence checklist

Market

- Size, by value and volume
- Segmentation e.g. customer group, supplier, product or service, channel, etc.
- Historic and forecast growth, by key segments
- Market drivers and restraints:
  - Customer requirements
  - Structure of customer base
  - Technology
  - Legislation/regulation
- Impact of economic variables, e.g. recession, population trends, interest rates, exchange rates, resource scarcity
- Recent and likely changes in competitive environment (e.g. consolidation, restructuring, diversification)
- Distribution channels and routes to market
  - Structure
  - Relative power of channel members
  - Recent and likely changes (e.g. direct sales, etc.)
- Alternative business models (e.g. low cost versus high service)

- Sources of competitive advantage: critical success factors, by segment or business model
- Impact of current market trends on margins

Products and services

- Description of competitive offerings
- Role in the value chain
- Competitive and substitute products and services
- Role of complementary products and services
- Alternative applications for products and services

Customers

- Overall customer segmentation
- Profiles of key customers or customer groups
  - Ownership
  - Size
  - Summary financial information
  - Main activities
  - Purchasing patterns
- Drivers of need for the product or service
- Importance of the product/service to the customer
- Purchase criteria:
  - Quality/performance
  - Price
  - Technical support
  - Customer service
  - Delivery
  - Relationship
  - Product bundling/package
  - Availability of stock/speed of response
  - Availability of spare parts/service
- Changes in purchasing power

- Purchase decision process, including timescales, people involved and external influencers or specifiers
- Single-supplier versus multiple-sourcing

The target company

- Overall business mix
- Organizational structure
- Outline financial performance, reasons for anomalies
- Assessment of product and market strategy
- Sources of competitive advantage
- Analysis of performance against industry critical success factors
- Strengths and weaknesses of key products and services
- Market positioning versus competitors, by segment
- Analysis of performance against customers' key purchase criteria (KPC)
- Relationships with key customers or customer groups
  - History
  - Quality
  - Substainability
- Effectiveness of sales and distribution channels
- Relationships with key suppliers
- Other external perceptions of the business
- Benchmark of key performance indicators (KPIs) against competitors (sales/productivity per employee, etc.)
- Quality of senior management
- Dependence on key management
- Staff turnover levels
- Reasons for departure of key staff
- External perceptions of operational management
- Relationship with current owner, any advantage or disadvantage brought

Competitors

- Ownership
- Structure

- Main activities
- Size, overall and for key product areas
- Financial performance
- Product and service analysis, likely developments
- Customers and segments served
- Performance compared to customers' key purchase criteria (KPC), compared to the target company
- Strengths and weaknesses
- Sources of competitive advantage (e.g. reputation, captive resources, critical relationships, etc.)
- Performance compared to industry critical success factors (CSF). Competitor's benchmarked to the target company
- Commitment to each market area
- Future intentions and strategy, likely reaction to market developments
- Strategic group analysis

New entrant analysis

- Possible entrants
- Barriers to entry
- Substitute products and services

Risk analysis

- Key risks
  - Likelihood
  - Impact
  - Mitigation

Forecast revenue analysis

- Management/vendor forecasts
  - Comparison to historic
  - Comparison to market
  - Comparison to competitive strength
  - Revised forecast

Gross margin analysis

- Management/vendor forecasts
  - Comparison to historic
  - Comparison to market
  - Impact of margin drivers on business
  - Revised forecast

Key post acquisition development actions

- Product/service enhancements
- Market positioning
- Pricing policy
- Distribution/channel policy changes
- Operational improvements
- Management strengthening
- New market or segment entry opportunities
- Fit with other businesses in the group
  - Cross-selling
  - Cost reduction/operating efficiencies

Exit analysis (private equity transactions only)

- Potential suitors
  - Current players
  - New entrants
- Suitability as exit partners
  - Strategic intent
  - Fit
  - Financial resources
- Barriers
  - Anti-trust
  - Other

Conclusions

- Single-page summary of key issues
- SWOT
- Forecast analysis (compared to business plan)
- Fit with acquirer's requirements
- Post-acquisition actions

Analysis

Commercial due diligence has a number of similarities to a standard strategy or strategic marketing review which would be carried out prior to launching a new product, or determining the future strategic direction of a business unit. Hence, it is not surprising that commercial due diligence employs many of the techniques and tools used in marketing and strategic reviews. A selection of them is mentioned here.

SWOT analysis

A well considered SWOT – a review of the company's *strengths, weaknesses, opportunities* and *threats* – is very valuable. It is rare for a commercial due diligence exercise to forego the use of a formal SWOT analysis. To be useful, the SWOT should mention only those aspects of a business which are important and relevant to its performance against its competitors. It should also avoid being too long; if it becomes a mere description of the company, it loses its analytical power (Figure 6.1).

Like other tools, a SWOT analysis is an aid to thought, so it is dangerous to be too prescriptive about it. In general, however, the strengths and weaknesses are internal to the company (concerned with its people, abilities and products) and are apparent in the present. The threats and opportunities are external (to do with the market and the competition) and concerned with the future.

Fig 6.1	Using SWOT analysis to assess attractiveness

Strengths	Weaknesses
Current strengths of the business for which the acquirer is prepared to pay. These attributes are methods of generating profits now and in the future and of creating value.	Current weaknesses of the business. Often they can be overcome, at a cost, by management action or investment. Ideally, the acquirer will have skills and resources which can counter key weaknesses; these are synergies.
Opportunities	**Threats**
Areas of growth or opportunities for future growth, given suitable management action or investment. Again the acquirer should bring skills and resources which will make some of these opportunities easier to achieve.	Issues beyond the control of the company which could damage its position and performance. It is important to assess the scale of these threats and the likelihood of them occurring. It is important also to consider what actions can be taken to mitigate the impact of the threats.

Source: AMR International

Key purchase criteria

Customers evaluate suppliers before purchasing, but it is not always clear to suppliers what their customers' key purchase criteria (KPCs) are. Customer requirements may also vary from market segment to market segment, and even from customer to customer. This underlines the importance of segmenting the market accurately, as well as understanding precise customer needs.

For example, the various customers of a removal company may have very different criteria. Some may think mainly about price, and if the odd book or piece of cutlery is lost or damaged that is less important than the money saved. For other customers the critical thing is that every possession arrives intact and price is a lesser concern. For others again, the process of moving is so stressful that the most important part of the service is simply the quality of service – the courtesy and the apparent concern for a smooth operation.

Table 6.2	Key purchase criteria of a removals company by customer type
Customer type	*Key purchase criterion*
Price-driven	Lowest price
Possession-driven	Avoidance of damage or loss
Stress-driven	Evident concern and consideration

Table 6.3	Relationship between KPCs and CSFs in the bicycle market		
Segment	*Low end*	*Mid range*	*Premium*
Key purchase criteria	1. Price 2. Availability 3. Fashionable	1. Quality 2. Brand 3. Price	1. Performance 2. Design/innovation 3. Brand
Strategy *(Value propositions)*	Low-end bikes sold through department and discount stores under retailer's own brand	Medium-price bikes sold primarily through specialist retailers under manufacturer's brand	High-price bikes for enthusiasts
Critical success factors	• Global sourcing and low-wage assembly • Supply contracts with major retailers • Supply chain efficiency	• Cost efficiency • Reputation for quality • Distribution	• Quality of components and assembly • Innovative design • Reputation and brand management
Key performance indicators	• Cost per unit • Growth in number of outlets • Average inventory level	• Cost per unit • % returns • Time to order	• % of defective bikes • Customer satisfaction rating • Brand awareness level

Source: AMR International

Within each group the purchase criteria should, of course, be further broken down.

A wise company will seek to understand the requirements of each customer, and insofar as is practicable it will tailor its products and services accordingly.

Critical success factors

Critical success factors (CSFs) define what a company must get right to achieve its goals and fulfil its strategy. They are therefore internal. As they are 'critical', there should not be too many of them.

For example, the CSFs for a sportscar company would include R&D, engineering excellence and branding. These deliver the performance and reputation required by the customer. Similarly, the CSFs for the family car company would include wide distribution, quality management and marketing in order to deliver price, reliability and resale value.

Table 6.3 shows the links between key purchase criteria and critical success factors as applied to a certain market.

Forecast analysis

A critical element of CDD is to provide a clear opinion on the target company's forecasts and how achievable they are.

The simple way to analyse forecasts is to establish growth in the relevant market segments and then to review the variance between the target's forecast growth rate and that of the market. Then it is useful to use a critical success factor analysis to bridge any gaps. If the business has an above average performance against critical success factors for the industry, then it can be expected to outperform the market. Conversely, if it is below average on its CSF performance then any claim to out-perform the market is difficult to believe.

Figure 6.2 shows a simple way of comparing the market to a company's sales. In the case illustrated by Figure 6.2 the market is highly cyclical, dipping in 2004 before recovering in 2006. Management forecasts show Product A to be underperforming in the market before gaining share in 2005 and 2006. Product C does the opposite, at first winning share before then falling back. The market investigations, and particularly customer interviews, did not support these swings in market share. The acquirer revised the forecasts and consequently the valuation of the business.

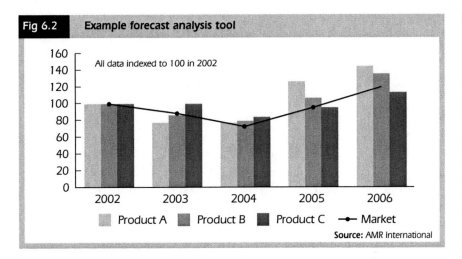

Fig 6.2   **Example forecast analysis tool**

All data indexed to 100 in 2002

Product A   Product B   Product C   → Market

Source: AMR International

Porter's five forces

Harvard Business School Professor Michael Porter has developed a useful *aide-mémoire* for deciding which aspects of a company's environment to analyse: the five forces model, M.E. Porter (1980), *Competitive Strategy: Techniques for Analyzing Industries and Competitors*, published by the Free Press.

The five forces are:

1. Competitive rivalry. Some markets have intense, sustained competition (air travel, PCs) others are less competitive (funeral services).
2. Buyers. As customers increase in size and markets globalize, the increased purchasing power of buyers can weigh heavily on smaller or less competitive companies. Carmakers and supermarkets are well known for their ability to leverage their buying power.
3. Substitutes. A company's entire business can be undermined by the arrival of substitutes. For example, the impact of the Internet may have been over-hyped in the short term, but travel agents are experiencing its threat on the medium- and long-term.
4. Suppliers. Businesses require a reliable, economic and consistent supply of goods and services. Any change in the availability or bargaining power of suppliers can be detrimental to a business.
5. Potential entrants. The arrival of significant new entrants can disrupt the status quo. Any software provider will worry if Microsoft starts eye its market niche at all seriously.

One useful way to use the five forces is to take each force and analyse its change over time. This analysis allows you to form a view about how market attractiveness has evolved and, more importantly, how it will evolve.

Case study – Snapple

Snapple was founded in Brooklyn, New York to supply ready-to-drink tea and juice drinks. The company grew fast in the 1980s and was floated in 1992. In 1994 Quaker Oats, the US cereal giant paid US$1.7 bn for the business. Quaker already owned Gatorade, a sportsdrink business with a turnover of US$1.2 bn. Snapple's sales at the time were US$700 m. Quaker believed that combining the two businesses would create valuable synergy by boosting the marketing muscle of each. It also sought to achieve sustained operational improvements.

In 1995 Snapple's sales fell 8%, and the business made an operating loss of US$85 m. Standard and Poor's downrated Quaker's bonds from A1 to A2, and Quaker's chief executive received no pay award for the year.

Quaker overlooked three things about Snapple's business which a thorough commercial due diligence exercise might have highlighted. First, the combined business' major competitors were not prepared to sit on the sidelines and allow a new force to emerge on their markets. Pepsi Co and Coca Cola attacked Snapple's market with new soft drink launches and by targeting key distributors.

Second, Quaker was seduced by the promising early results of a major export drive into Europe. Had it looked deeper it would have found that the importers had ordered large stocks but they were not moving through the distribution channels. Snapple and its agents had overestimated the product's potential and underestimated the effectiveness of the resistance from established brands like Fruitopia, Still Tango and Oasis and the clout of their respective distributors Food Brokers, Britvic and Coca-Cola Schweppes Beverages. Snapple failed to build the European consumer franchise that its original projections anticipated – and for which Quaker Oats paid so handsomely.

Third, there is an enormous cultural gap between Quaker and Snapple. Quaker is a serious type of business, while Snapple was a lively, rebellious, market and marketing-led company. The combination of the two businesses was an unhappy one. Quaker did not fully understand the product and market-based reasons for Snapple's success. It focused on financial and internal improvements and thereby severely undermined the basis for the business's success.

In 1997 Quaker sold Snapple to Triarc for US$300 m. Triarc reinvigorated product development and marketing, strengthened distribution, made some operational improvements and some small acquisitions. In 2000 it sold Snapple and some other softdrink brands to Cadbury Schweppes for US$1.45 bn.

Lessons learned: the analysis of a company's future cannot assume that competitors will not react to major events or move to fill market gaps. Equally, it is a mistake to assume that a product or business model which works in one country will succeed in another.

Trend charts

Trend charts show at a glance how the business is performing over time. They are designed for use when quantitative information is unavailable or unreliable, and are particularly useful when the business under review has a wide range of products and services.

A trend chart (Figure 6.3) tracking performance illustrates which areas are thriving, which are losing momentum, and which are struggling. A very powerful way to use trend charts is to show how the business performs against critical success factors (CSFs). The example below shows a trend chart for a trade show organizer.

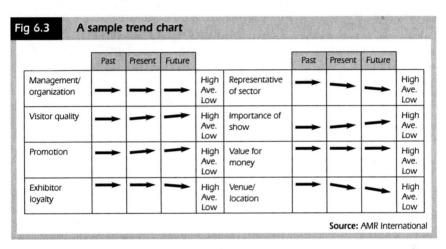

Fig 6.3   A sample trend chart

Source: AMR International

Perceptual maps

Perceptual maps help summarize and crystallize information and understanding. They can be used to illustrate the relative positioning of a range of competitors or products and can prompt decisions on the most promising course of action when a number of options are available.

A commonly used example is the market attractiveness/ability to compete chart (Figure 6.4). The attractiveness axis addresses issues such as the profitability of the existing competitors and the barriers to entry, while the ability axis shows the extent to which the company has the skills and resources needed to be a successful participant.

Another good example of perceptual mapping is strategic group analysis, which groups together organizations that have similar strategic characteristics, are following similar strategies or compete on similar bases. This analysis helps to identify the most direct competitors and any strategic gaps or opportunities. In particular, it highlights the difficulty of moving from one strategic group to another.

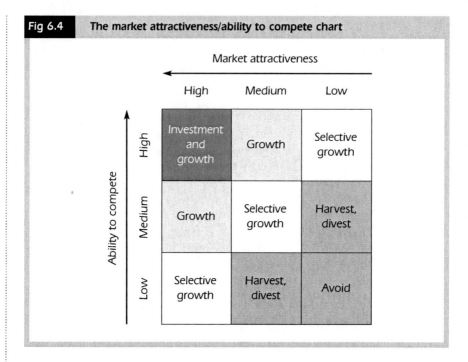

Fig 6.4   **The market attractiveness/ability to compete chart**

Some common characteristics to use for mapping strategic groups are:

- product or service diversity;
- geographical coverage;
- market segments served;
- channels used;
- degree or extent of marketing effort;
- extent of vertical integration;
- pricing policy;
- size;
- ownership.

Management assessments

Acquirers are now requesting increasingly informed opinions about management. Assessments of individual managers, and of the team as a whole, help acquirers to plan integration and organizational change by underlying the relative strangths and weaknesses of the team and its members.

There is no perfect way to obtain information on management and to analyse its quality and performance. The transaction process can restrict access and make formal assessments difficult. Although formal assessments, whether through depth interviews or psychometric tests, are the domain of human resource professionals more than the

> **The first part of any management assessment is to establish the relevant management skills required for each role in the business under the new ownership structure.**

commercial due diligence team, the commercial team can provide useful assessment information and some analysis.

The commercial team can report the views of various market participants obtained from external interviews, although these are limited to the market-facing managers they can be enlightening It can also report its view from the interviews with the target company's managers themselves. Again, as these meetings focus on the market and competitive position of the business, they will not cover all of the ground of a formal assessment. Nonetheless, a commercial team trained in the basics of management assessment can provide sufficient information for the acquirer to be forewarned of major management issues and challenges.

The first part of any management assessment is to establish the relevant management skills required for each role in the business under the new ownership structure. With these competence areas established, managers can be assessed according to their ability in each area.

A five- or seven-point scale in each performance area provides a good base for comparison. The scores on these scales are best backed up by evidence of performance in each area, as opposed to individual claims, hearsay or opinion. Assessments should also report individual strengths and weaknesses, or development areas for each manager.

As well as assessing individual managers, the team should be assessed as a whole. For example, a finance director who maintains a check on other more ebullient team members may hold the balance and any change would be detrimental. Alternatively, a stubborn and political finance director who blocks initiatives may damage team performance – and a change would help the business.

Styles and cultures

It is a commonplace observation that companies have different cultures. It is important to remember this when preparing the due diligence report. Cultures vary particularly between different countries; they also vary between different industries. But you do not have to travel from Mexico to Sweden or from the oil industry to the music business to observe stark differences of style and attitude. IBM and Microsoft are both in the computer business, both are significant players in the software industry, but their styles could hardly be more different. IBM has a traditional, formal culture, with echoes of its Quaker origins. Traditionally, its people wear blue suits, white shirts and dark ties. Microsoft's culture revolves around its still-young founder and its people see themselves as informal, casually dressed, unbureaucratic challengers of orthodoxy – even though other people in the industry worry about Microsoft's excessive dominance.

Numerous people have tried to analyse business cultures. Maslow and Hofstedter are among the most famous, but it is not necessary to apply rigid analytical tools to a discussion of culture. For practical purposes, we can all describe the differences between a British Airways, a Virgin Atlantic and an easyJet.

Numerous business people and academics have tried to analyse business cultures. Maslow and Hofstedter are among the most famous, but it is not necessary to apply rigid analytical tools to a discussion of culture. For practical purposes, we can all describe the differences between a British Airways, a Virgin Atlantic and an easyJet. The informal, even colloquial expressions we use are the tools that people will need if they are to attempt to integrate two or more cultures. The important thing is to assess the impact of any cultural differences on the integration process.

Who conducts commercial due diligence?

7

Commercial due diligence can be carried out by a range of people and organizations. The options are:

- the acquirer;
- an accountancy firm;
- a strategy consultancy;
- a market research firm;
- a commercial due diligence specialist;
- industry experts;
- no one.

There is no clear rule as to which is the 'right' organizsation to conduct CDD. Each organization has its positive and negative points. To an extent the type of organization selected for CDD depends on the individual circumstances of the acquirer – its resources, its self-confidence and the extent of shareholder vigilance.

A key point is trust. Acquirers or investors inevitably want to work with organizations they trust, and this comes down to people and relationships. If there is a positive relationship between a particular director or partner in a CDD firm and a client, then this counts for a lot. Acquirers and investors want to work with people whom they know will deliver.

The acquirer

Some private equity investors and frequent acquirers with substantial teams of professionals build up a great deal of in-house expertise about the CDD process, and so can carry out their due diligence in-house.

Advantages of doing it in-house

1: Cost

It is less expensive to use internal teams than consultants.

2: In-house expertise developed

The team should improve with every transaction as it builds up its experience. As well as getting better at the art and science of commercial due diligence, the team builds up an increasingly good understanding of which points are of paramount concern to the board members, and how to satisfy them.

3: In-built knowledge transfer

If the CDD is conducted by the acquirer itself, then it should not suffer any loss of information between the CDD work and the acquisition integration phase. Better still, if the managers who are to work in or alongside the newly acquired business conduct the CDD, then they are learning for themselves. However, it is essential for these future operational managers to have strong CDD skills and they must not form a biased view of their future companies.

4: Confidentiality

It is often argued that if only in-house people are involved, the chances of information falling into the wrong hands are reduced. In practice, this is a less powerful argument than the previous three: the professionals who carry out due diligence would be hopelessly compromised if they allowed vital information to slip out, and it is in fact more common for information to slip from in-house sources than from any other.

Disadvantages of doing it in-house

1: Insufficient resources

> It is often argued that if only in-house people are involved, the chances of information falling into the wrong hands are reduced. In practice, this is a less powerful argument than the previous three: the professionals who carry out due diligence would be hopelessly compromised if they allowed vital information to slip out.

Most companies do not have sufficient resources to establish a sufficiently large group of people specializing in due diligence work to cope with the intense workload of an acquisition.

2: Insufficient exposure

An in-house team lacks the benefit of working on a wide range of CDD cases. The team may also lack the wide range of skills needed to conduct CDD effectively. This can lead to less thorough analysis and to 'group-think' – the tendency to follow the lead of a dominant personality and remain blind to certain risks and dangers.

3: Loss of anonymity

Unless an in-house team goes to some length to disguise its identity, it will be unable to talk to market participants, especially competitors. In a non-auction process, the activities of the prospective acquirer may advertise its interest in the target company. This may provoke interest from other parties, and even raise the price of the target.

In a non-auction process, the activities of the prospective acquirer may advertise its interest in the target company. This may provoke interest from other parties, and even raise the price of the target.

4: Difficulty of saying 'no'

In extreme cases, the CDD team needs to confront the board or investment committee with bad news and this can lead to the deal being broken. In such cases it is best obviously for the business if the deal does not proceed, but the situation can become impossibly uncomfortable for staff members if a senior director is on the warpath and wants to push his pet project through.

Accountancy firms

The giant accounting firms offer commercial due diligence through their transaction services departments, which form part of their audit activities.

In recent years the management consultancy practices of the major accountancy firms have grown so fast that in some cases they have become larger than the accountancy practices they grew out of. Industry regulators and market events have consequently forced the major accounting firms to separate their management consulting activities from their audit arms. These now–separate firms sometimes use their industry groups and strategy consulting practices to carry out CDD projects.

The transaction services divisions of the audit arms of the accounting firms offer a range of corporate finance services along with financial and other types of due diligence. CDD is seen by many as the junior partner to the other main forms of due diligence as it has developed more recently, is less numbers based and earns lower fees. Nonetheless, after years of looking down their noses at CDD, the accounting firms have now woken up to its benefits and are starting to offer a service. This is hardly surprising as the links between FDD and CDD have become clearer and closer.

Advantages of using an accountancy firm

1: One-stop shopping

We have already seen how the best result is achieved through an exchange of information between the people doing commercial and financial due diligence. The CDD teams of the big accountancy firms argue that this is more effective if it takes place within one firm. With the entry of these firms into the legal arena, we are now hearing the argument that the whole due diligence process is best conducted by a single firm.

2: Resources

The accountancy firms are big and well-capitalized, with large numbers of hard-working, highly-qualified people working on a project. They have people who are expert in many – perhaps most – industries, and these people can be called on for advice and briefings. They have worldwide representation, and can staff a project in Belgium or Bolivia as well as in Basingstoke.

3: Brand names

The accountancy firms have reassuring brand names. Most chairmen feel they can trust their reports to be thorough and professional. And if a deal goes sour in the future, the acquiring management can at least argue that they employed a well-known, reputable firm to check the target business over.

4: Litigation targets

In extreme cases, the accounting firms make a target for legal recriminations. They have deep pockets, expensive professional indemnity insurance cover, and will go to great lengths to avoid their good name being besmirched. For example, KPMG paid tens of millions of dollars out of court to the shareholders of Ferranti for its part in the ISC fiasco (see case study on p. 33).

Disadvantages of using accountancy firms

1: Fear of litigation prevents frankness

The fact that the accountancy firms can be sued for misconduct can appear to be a significant advantage for the client. It is also a major argument against using them. In this increasingly litigious world, the audit firms are exercising ever greater care to avoid laying themselves open to misconduct or negligence suits. This means that they may decline to express an opinion if they cannot provide evidence to back it up. They may withhold information which is based on rumour and past experience rather than documentary proof.

Experienced clients will declare certain conversations with their audit-based advisers to be strictly off the record, but the courts have not always upheld that protection. In any case, clients may find themselves engaged in awkward negotiations about the limitations of liability before work begins.

Providing a valuable insight to one client about the competitive strategy of another (even if those two firms are not yet competitors) could – if discovered – jeopardize another consultancy or audit contract.

2: Conflicts of interest

Accountancy firms have a broad client base. While this gives them valuable contacts in most industries, it also gives them conflicts of interest. Providing a valuable insight to one client about the competitive strategy of another (even if those two firms are not yet competitors) could – if discovered – jeopardize another consultancy or audit contract. Partners within the services arm struggle with this issue on a daily basis, and it must at times diminish the value of their input into the decision-making process.

3: Talking to competitors

A yet more serious problem facing the accountancy firms is that they are sometimes unwilling to contact and talk to competitors. This is not the easiest thing to do, especially if you are perennially concerned about client conflict and about litigation. Nevertheless, on many commercial due diligence projects it is essential.

4: Insufficient market discussions

The accountancy firms employ people who have good commercial understanding – often they are accountants who have moved across into consultancy. But the firms' fee structures are such that it is difficult for their people to spend a lot of time talking to market participants.

Accountancy firms which recognize this sometimes subcontract an interview programme to a market research company. This is a poor substitute for doing the work in-house and, of course, it opens up the particular problems of doing this work through a market research firm.

5: Turf wars

The major audit firms may well have extensive geographical networks, hordes of industry experts and the ability to conduct both FDD and CDD. But turf wars between country offices and the different practice areas can cause problems.

Strategy firms

Strategy firms fall into two broad camps – the major strategy houses and the strategy 'boutiques'. The major strategy houses are the prestigious, established firms such as McKinsey, Booz-Allen Hamilton, Boston Consulting Group, and Bain and Co. The boutiques are the more recently established and smaller firms. There is more differentiation between the various strategy firms than between the audit firms, but for the purposes of this discussion they can be taken as a single group. Until the late 1990s strategy firms carried out much of the commercial due diligence work for the large financial investors – perhaps because they provide a training ground for many people in the financial sector. They also conduct strategy reviews for major corporates at the time of an acquisition – which is, in effect, commercial due diligence.

> **The boutiques are the more recently established and smaller firms.**

Advantages of using strategy firms

1: Resources

Like the accountancy firms, the strategy firms are well-capitalized, and have strength in depth. Many of them have offices all over the world, and they are able to staff very large projects. They also hire extremely talented people – the cream of the world's business schools are attracted to these firms by generous financial packages and by the chance to tackle complex problems for senior managers in large corporates, working with other very bright, stimulating professionals.

2: Rigour

They seek to apply great rigour to their work, using sufficient people on each project to go into tremendous detail on every aspect of the case.

3: Brand names

The strategy firms also boast superb brands. If a chairman of Acme Corporation can point to the support of McKinsey for the argument for taking over Roadrunner plc, he/she has a powerful weapon.

Disadvantages of using strategy firms

1: Cost

These high fee rates are harder to justify on a commercial due diligence exercise, unless the transaction is very large. Using a strategy consultancy on a commercial due diligence exercise is like using a sledgehammer to crack a nut.

The primary argument against using a strategy firm for commercial due diligence work is the expense. Their fee rates are commensurate with the premium intellectual horsepower of their consultants and the difficulty of the projects they are usually called on to undertake. These high fee rates are harder to justify on a commercial due diligence exercise, unless the transaction is very large. Using a strategy consultancy on a commercial due diligence exercise is like using a sledgehammer to crack a nut.

2: Commitment

Some strategy houses see commercial due diligence as 'low-end part-work'. Bright people join the strategy firms to grapple with detailed analyses of major corporate issues – changing the culture of an oil company, say, or restructuring a failing conglomerate. These are long-term, leading-edge, life-or-death business problems, and far removed from the cut-and-thrust of commercial due diligence work. The firm may well allocate the 'B' team to a CDD exercise.

3: Academic results

Some CDD clients of strategy firms complain about the limited practical nature of the results delivered. In some cases the consultants will have relied on management for much of their information and will have conducted just a handful of discussions with market participants. Some firms conduct these discussions with market participants in-house – and do them extremely well. Others believe this process is best done by others – often by market research companies.

Market research and marketing firms

Market research firms offer excellent interviewing skills, typically based on a qualitative approach. Some offer qualitative interviewing, including focus groups.

A number of marketing consultancies operate at a more analytical level, and deal with the whole spectrum of the marketing mix. Some of these term themselves business development consultancies or strategic marketing consultancies in order to avoid confusion with the mainstream type of marketing consultancy, which focus on the promotional aspects of the marketing mix.

They design and carry out research programmes, and help clients analyse the changing nature of their markets. They make recommendations as to how companies should address the market by improving the performance of existing products in existing markets, launching new products into existing markets, and entering new markets or categories. They advise on product and service performance levels and design issues, evaluate pricing strategies, assess which are the best distribution channels for a product and how to manage those channels, and help develop brand positioning strategies. These skills are relevant to commercial due diligence.

Advantages of using market research firms

1: Cost

In comparison with the alternatives, and especially the strategy firms, market research and marketing firms can offer an inexpensive way to carry out commercial due diligence.

2: Willingness to conduct interviews

Market research firms do not shy away from talking to large numbers of people in the market: indeed that is their bread and butter. They should provide a clear view of customer satisfaction.

Disadvantages of using market research firms

Quantitative market research requires that the question set is established at the start of the programme. It will be tested to ensure it does not offend respondents or generate totally irrelevant information, but after that it is fixed, otherwise the quantitative analysis loses its validity.

1: Depth of understanding

The problem with market research firms in the context of commercial due diligence is a lack of analysis and understanding. Quantitative market research requires that the question set is established at the start of the programme. It will be tested to ensure it does not offend respondents or generate totally irrelevant information, but after that it is fixed, otherwise the quantitative analysis loses its validity.

This approach is unhelpful in the context of commercial due diligence, where issues inevitably emerge and evolve as the programme proceeds.

The Market Research Society forbids its members to contact competitors of clients during projects.

Qualitative market researchers avoid this pitfall, but few, if any, have the profound understanding of how companies and markets operate, which would allow them to analyse the significance of what the market participants are telling them. In this sense they are the mirror image of the accountancy firms: they have no problem cold-calling a large number of market participants, but they lack the market understanding and analytical skill to transform the data they gather into usable intelligence. It would be rare to find a qualitative market researcher or marketing expert willing or able to respond with a straightforward answer to the question, 'Should we buy this company?'.

2: Talking to competitors

The Market Research Society forbids its members to contact competitors of clients during projects, arguing that it is unethical to do so. Not all marketing and market research firms abide by this injunction, but most do.

Commercial due diligence specialists

There is only a handful of specialist commercial due diligence firms. These firms have their roots firmly in strategy, marketing and research – the fundamental skill sets required of commercial due diligence providers.

Advantages of using due diligence firms

1: Speed

Specialists in commercial due diligence build up a level of expertise in accessing market participants and obtaining the required information in the fastest and most efficient way. As their core business is CDD, they are used to working on a series of short-term contracts.

Being small firms, the commercial due diligence specialists can, in a manner of speaking, go 'underneath the radar'.

2: The best of both worlds

Commercial due diligence specialists combine the research horsepower of the market researcher with the analytical skills of the strategy firms – without the fee levels of the latter. CDD firms have the specialist skills needed to conduct CDD.

3: Flexibility

Being small firms, the commercial due diligence specialists can be flexible in approaching market participants. They can, in a manner of speaking, go 'underneath the radar'.

Disadvantages of using due diligence firms

1: Brand name

Small commercial due diligence practitioners lack the brand name of a strategy house or an audit firm. The chairman may not be able to use the report as effectively as a defence against any complaints from angry shareholders after a deal has gone wrong. If the primary aim of carrying out commercial due diligence is to demonstrate in advance that appropriate precautions were taken, then commissioning a relatively unknown consultancy may not be the best option.

2: Resources

A small specialist commercial due diligence firm may not have the resources in-house to investigate a very large deal – especially one which requires work to be carried out in a large number of countries. Some of them have multilingual staff and networks of associates in many countries, but many clients do not find this approach as reassuring as working with a firm with a set of subsidiary offices.

3: Sector skills

Finally, a small specialist commercial due diligence firm may lack expertise in certain industry sectors. Some acquirers regard industry expertise as an absolute prerequisite for carrying out commercial due diligence, arguing that in only a few weeks it is very difficult for a team of consultants which has not worked in a particular industry before to learn enough about how that industry works to be able to evaluate a company's prospects.

This may be true in some industries which are particularly complex, or particularly fast-moving, such as computers or telecoms. But it is the current issues which arise in a commercial due diligence that matter –

> **It is the current issues which arise in a commercial due diligence that matter – prior industry knowledge is not always essential.**

prior industry knowledge is not always essential. In any event, CDD firms bring in industry experts to bolster their teams as necessary. The CDD methodology is often more important than industry experience.

Industry experts

Industry experts include retired managers seeking consultancy work and industry-focused consulting groups. They are sometimes called on for commercial due diligence work due to their industry knowledge and experience.

Advantages of using industry experts

1: Knowledge of the industry

Industry experts do not need to go up to the learning curve. They already know the sector and they know the participants. Their knowledge and contact lists should make for a simpler process and a better result.

2: Cost

A retired industry manager is much less expensive to hire than a consultancy firm.

Disadvantages of using industry experts

1: Process skills

Industry experts lack the process and analytical skills of CDD experts. They may know about the industry but they struggle to translate this into relevant analysis which links directly into the investment case or acquisition plan.

2: Imprecise knowledge

A significant danger of using industry specialists is that they can rely too heavily on their not quite up to date knowledge and their contact books. For example, an automotive expert is unlikely to know the tow bar or precision pressings segments in detail. Vague contacts and out-of-date information can be very dangerous as they lead to misleading results.

No one

It can be tempting just to go with an in-house opinion and avoid the time and expense of commercial due diligence. This can only be justified on very small transactions. On larger deals it is the recipe for disaster. This is the approach which bankrupted Ferranti after its acquisition of ISC.

PART 2
Financial due diligence

Objectives of financial due diligence ░8░

General objectives

In the introduction to this book we describe the typical process for the purchase of a business and we note that the major part of any due diligence exercise typically occurs after the signature of a letter of intent, Heads of Agreement, or similar document. In common with other forms of due diligence, the financial due diligence investigation has general objectives which reflect the stage reached in negotiations – broadly the parties have reached agreement but, from the purchaser's point of view that agreement is to a considerable extent founded on high level information, which needs verification. The general objectives of a typical financial due diligence investigation can be summarized as follows.

- To help to confirm the acquisition strategy, which may be underpinned by the current financial strength and ongoing trading performance of the target company and in this case the financial due diligence investigation should focus particularly on these issues.

- To confirm the validity of financial information provided by the vendor, if this information has been relevant to the acquisition decision. The financial due diligence investigation should, of course, be planned to place emphasis on features of the target business which are key to the investment decision. Standard procedures will rarely be appropriate and for each transaction it will be necessary to tailor the investigation in the light of the key drivers of the transaction.

- To help to confirm the possibility of generating synergies between the target company and the acquirer, and to help to quantify their financial impact of them.

- To look ahead to the post-acquisition integration of the target company, identifying likely difficulties and solutions.

For a financial investigation to be fully powerful and pertinent, those conducting the investigation must be properly appraised of the context of the investigation. The investigation can then be carefully tailored to focus on those issues which are key to the acquisition process. No two acquisitions are wholly alike, and so no two investigations should be wholly alike.

> **At all times the financial due diligence investigation should be focused on the future; the investigation of past events is useful only if it provides an insight into the future.**

At all times the financial due diligence investigation, whilst frequently drawing on historical information, should be focused on the future; the investigation of past events is useful only if it provides an insight into the future.

Key issues

A financial due diligence investigation is focused on financial issues, and the most important of these usually fall into the categories of earnings, assets, liabilities, cash-flows, net cash or debt and management.

Earnings

The investigation will seek to assess the level of maintainable earnings of the target business because they usually provide a guide to the future performance of the business. An assessment of maintainable earnings is much more than the identification of non-recurring profit and loss items. To assess the level of maintainable earnings is to gain a thorough understanding of the entire business and its market.

Assets

The investigation will include a review of the business assets. Again, this review will have an eye on the future – it will look at accounting issues, but it should be more concerned with the nature of the assets, and their suitability for the business. The investigation should seek to understand whether the business is equipped with assets appropriate to carrying on its activities, ascertain the need to invest in improvements to the asset base, and identify any assets owned by the business but not necessary to the current and prospective business activities. The investigation may also seek to compare the market value of assets with their net book value. For example, low net book values may give a misleading view of the level of capital required by the business over the long term, and so may flatter the true maintainable earnings of the business. The investigation should give thought to

> **Low net book values may give a misleading view of the level of capital required by the business over the long term, and so may flatter the true maintainable earnings of the business.**

the ownership of the key assets. A sale and leaseback transaction may be an efficient way to release cash, indirectly helping to finance the acquisition itself.

Liabilities

The investigation of liabilities will tend to look for any liabilities which have not been disclosed, or of which the value has been underestimated. This part of the investigation tends to be more backward looking, but, of course, the key underlying objective is to assess the level of any unexpected future cash outflows.

Cashflows

The investigation will aim to understand the extent to which profits are not simply reflected as net cash inflows. An apparently profitable business which fails to generate any cash may raise concerns. But there may be good reasons for a failure to generate cash – the business may have invested heavily, or a business may be growing rapidly, with a resultant increased working capital requirement acting as a drain on cash. These are important issues, key to understanding the likely or possible future performance of the business, and also key to ensuring that, following any acquisition, the business is properly financed.

> **There may be good reasons for a failure to generate cash – the business may have invested heavily, or a business may be growing rapidly, with a resultant increased working capital requirement acting as a drain on cash.**

Net cash or debt

Businesses are typically valued free of cash and financial debt. The presence of cash or financial debt in a target may therefore be capable of having a direct impact on the transaction price. To assess the level of cash or financial debt is not always easy, and factors to take into account may include seasonality and the presence of financial debt instruments accounted for off balance sheet.

Management

Many aspects of a due diligence investigation will involve interaction with the management of the target. Just as with commercial due diligence, financial due diligence investigations often depend on extensive interviews and discussions with key members of the target's management team. Therefore, the financial due diligence team should be in a good position to express a view on the strengths and weaknesses of the management team. This can be of particular importance when planning for the integration of the target into the acquiring group, as it will often be necesssary to anticipate how the target's management team will need to be adjusted to take account of its new environment following completion of the acquisition.

Methods 9

arrying out a financial due diligence investigation involves obtaining information, often in a testing environment. The information may not be easy to come by. There may be deliberate attempts to stifle the flow of information. A sound strategy for obtaining information is therefore key to a successful investigation.

Financial due diligence typically differs from commercial due diligence in that the former concentrates on information available inside the target company. It differs from legal due diligence in that, being focused on information relevant to future performance, it inevitably admits information that is soft in nature. For example, financial due diligence may attach considerable weight to information obtained through interviews with key managers and other staff.

It is worth insisting on the relationship between financial and commercial due diligence. Their objectives may sometimes appear similar and there may seem to be duplication. But duplication is in fact rare. For example, both financial and commercial due diligence may seek evidence to support a target's ongoing market share. The commercial investigation will do this using information gained outside the target, and will seek to build up a picture of the perception of the target on its market, so giving a feel for how market share might evolve going forward. The financial investigation will use information available inside the target, including thorough interviews with managers and staff. This also will build towards a view of the target's relationship with its customers and its market. Frequent disagreements with major customers, evidenced through poor payment records, disputes on invoices, frequent credit notes, warranty claims, and related interviews with relevant staff and managers may cast doubt on the target's ability to retain its market share.

> **Both financial and commercial due diligence may seek evidence to support a target's ongoing market share.**

The scope of FDD

Defining the scope of a financial due diligence investigation is key to its success. The investigation must concentrate on areas that really are important. Quite apart from the waste of resource, time spent on unimportant issues may compromise other more crucial parts of the investigation and may even jeopardize negotiations by annoying the target's management and advisers. The scope of an investigation will depend upon the circumstances of each case. Some of the factors which will usually need to be taken into account will include:

- *The rationale for the acquisition or the deal strategy.* For example, the decision to invest may be very strongly driven by a truly exceptional opportunity to penetrate a new market. In this context the due diligence effort should be focused on confirming the size and solidity of the target's market share. Other commonly important factors, such as profitability and cash flows may be of secondary importance only. On the other hand, a leveraged transaction may be critically dependent on the level of free cash in the target at completion and on the subsequent ability of the target to generate further free cash.

- *The size of the target relative to the acquirer.* For a relatively small acquisition, a large acquirer may feel able to 'take a view' and effect limited due diligence only.

- *The activity of the target compared with the acquirer.* When making an acquisition in its own sector, an acquirer may feel comfortable with less thorough due diligence.

- *The principal country of the target compared with the acquirer.* When making an acquisition in a new country, an acquirer would usually be well-advised to effect thorough financial due diligence investigations.

- *Availability of information.* Increasingly, vendors seek to achieve control over the sale process, including placing limitations on the opportunity given to purchasers to perform due diligence. In such cases a buyer and its advisers will, of course, seek to maximize the opportunity to perform due diligence. However, it is also important to be realistic and to adapt the rest of the process in accordance with the opportunity to perform due diligence. It may be possible to cover many points in the sale and purchase agreement, and a vendor who has restricted the acquirer's due diligence process will often be in a weaker position when defending declarations and warranties.

The decision to invest may be very strongly driven by a truly exceptional opportunity to penetrate a new market. In this context the due diligence effort should be focused on confirming the size and solidity of the target's market share.

Choosing an adviser

It can be advantageous to perform financial due diligence in-house. The in-house team is likely already to have good knowledge of the industry sector, may have been close to the transaction from the earliest stages and so may easily be able to appreciate fully the strategy of the acquisition. But there are also clear advantages to be gained from subcontracting much of the financial due diligence investigation:

- Members of the subcontracted team should be financial due diligence specialists, spending all their time on transaction-related work. The financial due diligence team should therefore be used to all the difficulties of obtaining pertinent information, and capable of finding creative ways round those difficulties.

- The management of the target company may be very reluctant to allow access to managers from a competitor, but may be more easily inclined to allow access for an independent professional firm.

- The acquirer's own team may already be fully stretched. Subcontracting the financial due diligence investigation often assists in resolving a simple problem of resource.

- The financial due diligence investigation is only part of the wider acquisition process. To subcontract the financial due diligence allows the acquiring company's management to remain focused on the 'big picture', and to avoid becoming bogged down in too much detail.

Whilst it is often preferable to subcontract the financial due diligence investigation, it is always important to retain close communication between the financial due diligence team and its client. In this way the financial due diligence team can benefit from the industry expertise of its client and should also be close to developing the acquisition strategy.

Financial due diligence instructions

Care should be taken when instructing the financial due diligence team. Obvious perhaps, but this is easily overlooked in the pressed environment of many acquisitions. One or two points should particularly be looked at:

- *The instruction letter should pay careful attention to the scope of the work.* This should enable the acquirer to feel that the investigating accountants have really understood the acquisition strategy and so will indeed be concentrating on the issues that are important to the acquirer.

- *The timing and form of any reports should be set out clearly.* Preparing a full long-form report is a costly exercise and may not always be appropriate. The advantage of preparing a detailed formal report is that the required discipline forces the investigating accountants into giving careful consideration to all the results of their investigation. Also, the report itself can become a useful reference document giving a full description of the target company from a financial perspective. A set of powerpoint slides is usually a cheaper end product, but is likely to be less comprehensive.

- *Fee estimates.* It is common practice for advisers to invoice in accordance with their time spent, but to provide a fee budget which can only be exceeded with the client's prior agreement. However, a client should be prepared for a fee budget to be exceeded – it is usual to prepare a fee budget on the assumption that information will be freely available and that no particular difficulties will arise. The reality is rarely so simple and the very nature of acquisitions is such that the course of events is unpredictable.

- *Abort and success fees.* It is increasingly common practice for financial due diligence fees to depend on the successful completion of a transaction, with a reduction in the fee payable in respect of an aborted transaction, and an uplift in the fee in respect of a completed transaction. When agreeing this kind of arrangement care should be taken to avoid creating a situation in which the adviser has, or appears to have, a conflict. This is less likely to cause a problem in the case of an acquisitive client which effects several transactions each year using the same advisers.

Obtaining information

The investigating accountant will obtain information from a wide variety of sources, but almost always the sources of information will be internal to the target company.

> It is increasingly common practice for financial due diligence fees to depend on the successful completion of a transaction, with a reduction in the fee payable in respect of an aborted transaction, and an uplift in the fee in respect of a completed transaction.

Shopping lists

Prior to commencing a financial due diligence investigation it is common practice to provide the vendors and their advisers with a detailed information request list (or 'shopping list'). Firms experienced in conducting financial due diligence investigations will have standard shopping lists. In some circumstances, and to gain time, it may be appropriate simply to use a standard list, but in this case the vendors should be told that the list is standard and that it may therefore include irrelevant requests and exclude items important to the transaction in question. In such cases the vendors should be told that the standard list is designed to give a feel for the information that will be required and so to help broadly direct the vendors' preparation for the investigation.

> **Too many due diligence investigations get off to a bad start because the various advisers inundate the poor vendors with huge ill-considered requests for information, with much duplication across the different lists.**

Often it will be preferable to tailor the standard list to the circumstances of each particular transaction, in which case it will be important for the different due diligence teams to co-ordinate their work, such that the different information request lists overlap as little as possible.

Too many due diligence investigations get off to a bad start because the various advisers inundate the poor vendors with huge ill-considered requests for information, with much duplication across the different lists. Understandably, the vendors take this badly and, whether because genuinely annoyed or for tactical reasons, the vendors may then use such signs of poor preparation to put the purchaser on the back foot, trying to weaken his negotiating position.

Appendix B is an example of a shortened financial due diligence information request list.

Interviews with the target's management

A financial investigation will be based on documentary information and also on interviews. The interviews form a critical part of most financial investigations. They will often be based around documents, but the investigating accountant will also steer the conversation away from hard issues, always seeking to improve his understanding of the target business, its strengths and weaknesses, what it might aspire to and where it might prove vulnerable.

The investigating accountant may seek to cover similar ground with several different members of the target's management team. For example, it may prove interesting to compare the views of the managing director, finance director and production director.

It is important to understand the history of each interviewee. A newly recruited manager may be more ready to criticize a business with which he or she does not have a long historical association, while a longstanding manager may feel

It is important to understand the prospects of each interviewee. An owner-manager who has spent his entire career building his business, and who plans to retire immediately following the prospective sale, will naturally tend to present his business in a favourable light.

that any criticism of the business amounts to a criticism of him personally and it may be difficult for him to view the business objectively – but the detailed knowledge he will have acquired over the years may make him an invaluable source of information nonetheless.

It is important to understand the prospects of each interviewee. An owner-manager who has spent his entire career building his business, and who plans to retire immediately following the prospective sale, will naturally tend to present his business in a favourable light. No vendor is left untouched by the prospect of perhaps receiving a very substantial sum of cash that will secure his financial future for life. Some vendors remain entirely honest and fairly seek to present their business in the best possible light; some are prepared deliberately to conceal and fabricate information in order to secure a sale.

The prospects of a professional manager who is not a vendor and who is being 'sold with the business' are quite different. Such a manager may quite quickly 'change sides' and identify with the purchaser, his prospective employer. He may even be motivated to show the business in a poor light, in order that a good performance following the acquisition will be attributed to his subsequent good management.

There are, of course, many different scenarios. When a business is being sold, it is often a traumatic period filled with uncertainty for its managers and it is important that the investigating accountant be sensitive to the different circumstances of each transaction and each manager or interviewee. Interviews can then be tailored accordingly, and much valuable information wheedled out as a result.

The target's historical advisers

It is common practice for the investigating accountants to review the working papers of the auditors to the target, and to interview the auditors. The auditors will not necessarily allow access to their working papers. The target must formally give the auditors permission to open their files and the auditors will usually seek a hold harmless letter signed by the investigating accountants and their client to ensure that they cannot be held liable as a result of having provided access to their audit working papers. Legal advice should, of course, be taken before committing to any hold harmless undertaking and related indemnity.

From a practical point of view, it is worth bearing in mind that often the auditors will not open up their files quickly. Putting in place the hold harmless and related letters takes time and often involves some negotiation on the precise drafting. Sometimes no agreement is reached and the auditors refuse access to their working papers, in which case the purchaser and its advisers will have to manage otherwise, perhaps by extending the scope of their own investigations to include some pure audit work.

The auditors' working papers are reviewed for two reasons:

1 To get a feel for the quality of the audit, and so gain comfort that any clean audit opinions are supported by appropriate audit work.

2 To gain an initial understanding of the target company and its business (if the investigating accountant can review the audit papers before beginning his work at the target, he can then arrive at the target company with some basic knowledge and so go straight to more significant issues with the management of the company).

Similarly, it can be useful to have an exchange with the tax and legal advisers of the target company. If possible all this work with advisers to the target should precede the work carried out at the target. This initial work with the auditors and advisors helps to prepare for the crucial work at the target itself; and the better prepared the investigating accountant, the more likely he is to make a good impression at the target – and so to build a good constructive relationship with the management of the target.

Contents of a FDD investigation

In the following chapters the contents of a typical financial due diligence investigation are considered in some detail. Appendix A summarizes the topics typically covered by a FDD investigation

History and commercial activities **10**

Overview

A prime objective of any financial due diligence investigation will be to give a view on the level of maintainable earnings of the target, and on the quality of those earnings. Even where the investigation does not specifically include a review of forecast financial information, the underlying objective in reviewing historical information is to give an insight into the future potential of the business to generate profits.

A review of maintainable earnings necessarily involves reaching a thorough understanding of the business and its environment. Only in this way can the investigator begin to understand the extent to which the past performance of a business might be a guide to the future.

Investigating accountants concentrate on information available within a target. As already discussed, in seeking to understand the business the investigating accountants will rely extensively on interviews with the top management of the target, and also perhaps on more informal conversations with relatively junior staff.

Examples of issues which might arise on the investigation of a target's history and commercial activities include the following.

- *Changes in the shareholders.* Such changes may be benign, but could, for example, indicate that the founders fell out. Perhaps the remaining shareholders are difficult to live with; perhaps they will not easily fit into a group environment following the acquisition, and the business might suffer as a result. It will be worth letting the commercial due diligence team know of any departing shareholders as it may be useful to interview them.

- *Changes in the management.* Changes in the management may reveal personality issues, but might also reveal disagreements over strategy, and the outgoing managers may make useful interviewees for the commercial due diligence team.

> **It will be worth letting the commercial due diligence team know of any departing shareholders as it may be useful to interview them.**

> **It is not unusual to groom a company for sale, and a reduction in the rate of investment can be a good way to flatter profits, by reducing the depreciation charge.**

- *Insufficient investment.* It is not unusual to groom a company for sale, and a reduction in the rate of investment can be a good way to flatter profits, by reducing the depreciation charge. Reduced levels of investment will also flatter cashflows, and this at the expense of the future profitability of the business. A careful review over a number of years may reveal a decline in the level of investments. It can also be useful to interview managers on the production, or operational side of the business, as they may have been frustrated by a period of low investment.

- *Dependence on one or few key suppliers.* A business may have little choice over the suppliers it uses for some products, and this may render the business vulnerable to the behaviour of any such key suppliers. This may arise where for technical reasons a supplier cannot be avoided, but can also simply reflect the relative size of the supplier compared with the target business – in a sector where the suppliers are very large they may have a position of strength. Where a business is particularly dependent on one or few suppliers, the nature of the contractual arrangements in place with those suppliers will be of particular importance.

- *Similarly, dependence on one or few customers.* It will be important to understand why a business is dependent on few customers, and the extent to which it is realistic to aim to decrease such dependence. For instance, in some sectors it is common for a young company to depend on few large customers, but it is also a natural development for that dependence to become diluted simply through growth of the business.

- *The presence of 'change of control clauses' in key contracts.* Such clauses are quite common in debt and lease contracts, as well as in substantial supplier contracts. Their presence can be a two-edged sword: on the one hand, the contract may be crucial to taking the business forward, and any uncertainty surrounding the contract may be upsetting to the business; on the other hand, the change of control clause may open up the possibility of renegotiating key terms of the contract and so setting the business on a firmer footing.

- *Seasonality in the business.* Of course, an acquirer looking at a target in the same sector may be used to the seasonality, but a change of country may lead to a significant change in the pattern of any seasonality. Similarly, an apparently minor difference in the nature of the activity might result in different seasonality. The timing of a deal may be influenced by seasonality, as may the timing of any post-acquisition integration measures.

A change of country may lead to a significant change in the pattern of any seasonality. Similarly, an apparently minor difference in the nature of the activity might result in different seasonality.

- *Competitive threats* due to new investment by a competitor from another country.

- *Disputes with a major supplier.* Such a dispute may be revealed through interviews, or through observing that payments to the supplier are behind, or because the target business has changed to another supplier.

- *Problems of quality control.* Such difficulties may be revealed by a high level of credit notes, reflecting a high level of returns; or they may be revealed by a review of credit control – customers who are paying unusually slowly may not be happy with the service.

Case study – French retail chain

In this case the strong seasonality of the target business, typical of many retailers, was to play a critical role in the due dilligence process and in the related negotiations.

The target company was a French retail chain with sales of €30 million which had made good profits in previous years, but which was performing less well at the time of the financial due diligence investigation. Purchases were made from a small number of key suppliers, with no realistic opportunity to deal with any other suppliers. The suppliers operated a system whereby purchases were made at a price very near to the final retail selling price, and the retailer's margin came through substantially in the form of volume-related discounts. The rate of the discounts depended on the volume of purchases achieved over the full calendar year.

The target closed its accounts on 30 June, and the financial due diligence investigation took place in September. The level of rebates was critical to the profitability of the retailer, and the final amount of the rebates was not clear until about March following the relevant calendar year. Like many retailers, there was strong seasonality of sales, with much the strongest sales taking place in the run-up to Christmas.

Case study – French retail chain (continued)

The most recent accounts, for 30 June, included a provision for volume rebates, based on an estimate of purchase volumes for the full calendar year. Given the importance of the sales volumes (and so of the related purchases) at the end of the year, the estimate of purchase volumes was subject to considerable uncertainty, bringing into question the level of profitability of the business.

Investigation of the valuation of stocks also revealed that, contrary to previous years, stocks had been valued at gross purchase price, without taking into account the volume rebates. Closing stocks were therefore overvalued, with a resultant overstatement of profits. This further reduced the apparently weak profits.

The weak profits, together with the uncertainty of the level of the final rebates, left the acquirer feeling uncomfortable, particularly in view of the strongly seasonal sales, with the main pre-Christmas sales due just after completion of the deal. To resolve these difficulties the purchase consideration was renegotiated; the maximum possible consideration remained unchanged, but the part of the consideration dependent on the earnings of the target over the calendar year in progress was substantially increased. The deal was completed in October, leaving only a few months before the final price, dependent on the profits for the calendar year, was known, and so integration could soon begin without fear of a conflict between the short-term profit objectives of the vendors and the longer-term integration plans of the new owners.

Case study – European plant hire

The target was in the business of hiring out heavy plant and construction equipment, a highly capital-intensive activity. The profit trends over the last three years appeared excellent, with a steady and strong increase in profitability over the period. Cash generation was also good, with a positive trend broadly consistent with the improving profits.

The financial due diligence investigation revealed that the company used an accelerated method to calculate its depreciation charge, giving rise to a high charge in the early part of an asset's life. The total period over which the plant was depreciated was also quite short, with the result that some assets used in the business had a very low, or nil, net book value.

The investigation also showed that the level of capital expenditure on new plant had declined over recent years. As a result, the average age of the plant had increased and, due to the manner in which the depreciation charge was calculated, the depreciation charge for an essentially unchanged plant park had declined.

The apparent improvement in profits therefore reflected the accelerated calculation of the depreciation charge and the reduced level of investment in new plant; the true underlying performance of the business had not improved. And the improvement on cash generation merely reflected the reduced investment in new plant.

Organizational structure and employees **11**

The investigating accountant should focus on the role of the management and employees in ensuring the success of a business. This review should be complementary to that of the legal due diligence team, which will focus more on the contractual relationships with management and employees.

An investigation might reveal significant issues regarding the management of a company, such as the following:

- *A high degree of dependence on a key general manager.* In this case it may be appropriate to take steps to tie the key manager into the business, with a suitably motivating package and a non-compete agreement, perhaps including an earnout if the key manager is a major vendor. If the key manager does not intend to stay with the business for more than a short while, it may be appropriate to initiate a search for a suitable successor.

- *A high degree of dependence on a specific person*, such as an IT manager or the leader of a research and development team. Even though such a person may not be particularly senior in the organization, his or her departure could perhaps cause significant disruption and loss of value.

- *The recent loss of a key manager.* This may cause immediate difficulties to the business, but may also be worth investigating for what else it may say about the business or its market. The investigation should seek to explain why the target was unable to retain the key manager. Perhaps the manager's departure arose following a disagreement on strategy, or perhaps the manager believed that the target business would soon be in decline.

- *Significant weaknesses in the management team.* An owner-managed business might, for example, have a relatively weak finance and administration function, which a corporate or financial buyer might want to strengthen. The purchaser might wish to instruct an executive search firm to look for a suitable finance director even while the due diligence process is still in progress.

- *A culture very different from that of the acquirer.* Following an acquisition a clash of cultures may be harmful and difficult to manage.

> **The investigation should seek to explain why the target was unable to retain the key manager.**

- *Duplication with the acquirer's management team.* In which case, even at the due diligence stage of the transaction, it may well be appropriate to plan for how any such duplication will be best dealt with following completion of the transaction.

The financial due diligence investigation might reveal issues of the following nature in relation to the employees:

- *The target may make extensive use of overtime work.* This may not be sustainable in the long term. Increasing the headcount may improve short-term profitability, but will increase the fixed cost base and so increase risk.

- *There may be a shortage of suitable skilled workers* and this might restrict the potential for growth of the business.

- *The workforce may be strongly unionized.* The reaction of the unions to a change in ownership may be difficult to predict. In any event the profitability of the business may be dependent on avoiding industrial action.

- *There may be a high level of staff turnover*, and this in turn may reflect other weaknesses in the business.

- *Rates of pay or other conditions of employment in the target may be significantly different from those of the acquirer.* During the integration process, following completion of the acquisition, it may be difficult to resist pressure to bring all staff up to a similar remuneration package, so increasing the cost base of the combined business.

- The acquirer may believe that the acquisition will give rise to economies of scale which can be realized only through redundancies. As part of the due diligence process it will then be appropriate to investigate where the redundancies should be made, what the associated costs will be, and what procedures must be followed to effect the redundancies. In some countries it may be difficult to make redundancies, and this will need to be investigated carefully.

Case study – executive search

The target was an executive search business. Key to the success of the business was the ability to retain the consultants, who tended to have close relationships with clients. There was a risk that any consultants leaving the company might take their clients with them. The manner in which the consultants were remunerated was therefore critical, the remuneration package being designed to ensure that the consultants shared appropriately in the business which they brought to the company and also shared appropriately in the business which they handled.

The acquirer used a remuneration system for consultants which gave the consultants a proportion of the fee income they won for the company and a share of the fee income they actually handled. The target used a different system, much more dependent on giving the consultants an equity stake in the target company.

A crucial part of the due diligence investigation was to understand the remuneration system operated by the target, and to assess how the consultants of the target could be brought into the acquirer's system, but without causing disruption to the two businesses.

Case study – French blanket manufacturer

The target was a French blanket manufacturer. During the due diligence process it became clear that, whilst the target's accounting systems complied with French statutory requirements, the accounting function of the target fell some way short of the requirements of the UK acquirer, which was quoted on the London Stock Exchange. For example, the target produced very little monthly management accounting information, and produced its annual statutory accounts about four months after the year end.

It was clear that, following completion of the acquisition, the acquirer would need to strengthen the target's finance function as a matter of urgency. This would be essential in order to comply with the group requirements for a full monthly management accounts pack on the second Monday of each month. Moreover, the management accounts pack needed to comply with UK accounting practices, whereas the target's current team had experience of preparing information in accordance with French accounting practices only.

Upon identifying this issue, the acquirer began its search for a suitable British financial controller, who would work for the target's existing French finance director. Following completion of the deal, and in the interim period before the British financial controller was recruited, the acquirer seconded a member of its UK finance team to support the new French subsidiary.

Information systems and accounting policies **12**

Information systems

The quality of a company's information systems underpins its ability to report its trading performance accurately, and affects the company's ability to safeguard its assets and to record fully its liabilities.

The financial investigation of a company with weak information systems is likely to prove difficult, may overshoot deadlines, and will almost certainly be more expensive than the investigation of a similar company with strong information systems. Strong information systems also give confidence in the business as a whole.

Typically a company with strong information systems will be tightly managed in accordance with carefully drawn-up plans.

Typically a company with strong information systems will be tightly managed in accordance with carefully drawn-up plans.

Accounting policies

An important part of a financial investigation is the review of the accounting policies. This is usually true even where the scope of the investigation has otherwise been limited.

The reported profits of a business can depend very significantly on the accounting policies adopted by that business. And the interpretation of the accounting policies can also be used to give flexibility without apparently changing the accounting policies. The investigating accountant will therefore need to investigate carefully any changes to accounting policies and, less easy to do, he will also need to look into any changes in the application of ongoing accounting policies.

In an international environment the importance of the review of accounting policies becomes greater. Different countries adopt different accounting practices, and this can lead to significant differences in reported results. A potentially crucial issue is the fact that different countries use different definitions of financial debt for accounting purposes. This can have a simple and direct effect on the price payable for a target where the price is negotiated free of cash and of financial debt.

Some examples of issues that can arise on the review of accounting policies and information systems include:

- *The approach to the recognition of income on long-term contracts*. Different companies may adopt different accounting policies for the recognition of income on long-term contracts. Even in the case of companies which apparently have similar accounting polices for long-term contracts, it may be that a detailed investigation will reveal significant differences.

- *Depreciation rates for similar assets may vary significantly from company to company.*

- *Provisions against investments, including goodwill.* The decision to provide against an asset may often necessarily include a strong element of subjective judgement, and an acquirer may not feel comfortable with the approach adopted by a target company. Similar considerations apply in the review of provisions against any contingent liabilities.

Stocks might be valued on the basis of the most recent purchase invoice, or using a calculation of an average purchase price over a period of time.

- *Stock valuation.* In the case of a trading company, the valuation, of stock may be relatively simple, but even then different estimates may be used and may feed through to the level of profits. For example, stocks might be valued on the basis of the most recent purchase invoice, or using a calculation of an average purchase price over a period of time. In the case of a manufacturing company, the valuation of stock is much more complex, and the methods used to absorb direct and indirect production costs into the valuation of stock will be capable of having a significant impact on the final stock valuation and, therefore, the declared profits.

A company looking to report a good level of profits may seek to reduce the level of provision in order to flatter profits.

- *The level of provision against slow-moving or obsolete stocks and against slow-paying trade debtors admits of subjective judgement.* A company looking to report a good level of profits may seek to reduce the level of provision in order to flatter profits. An investigating accountant will seek to identify any such attempt to 'manufacture' profit.

Case study – European transport and logistics

In this case a deal was negotiated based on a debt free price for the target. Differing accounting practices, together with market seasonality, made it difficult to agree what the debt free price meant in terms of a price actually payable by the aquirer for the target's equity.

The target was a logistics and transport company with significant seasonal variations in the volume of its business. Heads of Agreement had been signed and included an indicative price clause where the parties had agreed to an enterprise value, free of cash and financial debt, and had agreed therefore that the final consideration payable would be adjusted in the light of the level of cash or financial debt in the target group at completion.

Two issues arose in this respect in the course of the financial due diligence investigation:

1 The target group had accounted for certain lease contracts in respect of trucks 'off balance sheet'. This means that these leases were accounted for as simple rental contracts, with the monthly rental simply being accounted for as a profit and loss account charge, and with no asset or financial debt being accounted for on the balance sheet. A review of the lease contracts showed that under UK accounting rules these were finance leases which would therefore be accounted for 'on balance sheeet', with the trucks being shown as an asset in the balance sheet, and with corresponding financial debt also being shown as a liability, like a bank loan, in the balance sheet. The UK treatment increases the level of financial debt, and so, under the terms of the Heads of Agreements, directly resulted in a lower purchase consideration.

2 When signing the Heads of Agreement the acquirer had not fully appreciated the seasonal nature of the target business. The financial due diligence review showed there to be significant seasonality, with a substantial impact on the level of cash in the business. Completion was scheduled to coincide with a peak in the cash position and, under the Heads of Agreement, terms this meant that the consideration would be increased because of this temporarily favourable cash position.

In the light of these findings the acquirer renegotiated the terms of the deal. The off-balance sheet leases were treated as financial debt, so reducing the consideration payable, but the debt free price was increased to reflect the improved profits before interest and tax once the leases had been

Case study – European transport and logistics (continued)

brought on to the balance sheet. The net effect was to reduce the purchase consideration significantly.

The seasonality of the cash position was more complex to deal with. The final price clause included an adjustment designed to reduce the price in order to eliminate the effect of the seasonal peak in the cash position at completion. The adjustment sought to measure an underlying average free cash position over the year adjusted to eliminate the seasonal variations.

Case study – French forge

In this case the valuation of stocks was unclear, but was critical to measuring the profitability of the target company.

The target was a forge, making heavy duty steel products. The nature of the business required a significant investment in stocks. The target was making good profits and so the owner-manager had felt comfortable carrying a very significant holding of stock. The high level of stock also allowed the owner-manager to influence the target's accounting profits by making adjustments to the year end accounting stock figure.

In the past the owner-manager had not been greatly concerned with a precise measure of the business' profits – to see that the business was clearly making good money was sufficient for his ongoing management needs. In the context of the sale of the business, and of a valuation based on earnings, a precise measure of profits became crucial. In assessing the true maintainable earnings of the business the valuation of stock was therefore a sensitive issue. The vendor produced historical profit and loss accounts which he believed to reflect the true underlying earnings of the business.

The valuation of stocks was necessarily complex. The precise manner in which the very significant direct and indirect costs of production were absorbed into stock could have a substantial effect on the final valuation of stock and so on in profits. The vendor's historical profit and loss accounts used an outdated system for absorbing production costs, this system being based on the production process as it functioned some 20 years earlier. Further investigation suggested that the valuation system in fact underabsorbed production costs into stocks, resulting in an undervaluation of stocks.

Since the amount held in stock had been increasing over the period of the historical profit and loss accounts, the systematic undervaluation of stocks had resulted in an understatement of profits.

The buyer was therefore reassured because, although the accounting records of the target were not perfectly clear, the financial due diligence investigation suggested that the target was in fact making more profit than that declared by the vendors.

Trading results **13**

The financial review of the trading results draws on other areas of the financial investigation and, above all, will depend on a thorough understanding of the business of the target.

Sales, costs of sales, gross margins

The review of trading results should typically concentrate on sales, cost of sales and gross margins. This is where the figures reflect the nub of the business, and where the value in the target is concentrated – in its capacity to generate gross margins. The review of sales and gross margins will seek to understand the main underlying trends in the performance of the business. It will identify any factors having a non-recurring impact on performance and will quantify the impact of such non-recurring events. In attempting to understand the forces driving the business, the review will also aim to identify any key success factors which perhaps may not be relied upon in the future. The information produced by this review should give a good feel for the quality, or repeatability, of the sales and gross margins of the business. Armed with this information the investigating accountant and his client will be well-placed to form a view on how the business might perform in the future.

The review of the sales and gross margin should identify the key uncertainties on which the performance of the business depends. For example, sales might depend on the weather, or gross margins might be dependent on movements in commodity prices.

The review of overheads is typically easier to effect and is perhaps of secondary importance compared to the review of sales and gross margin. Here the investigator will seek to gain a full understanding of the overhead base. The review will involve explaining variations from year to year and, in particular, will seek to identify any exceptional items as well as any ongoing changes

> **The investigator will seek to gain a full understanding of the overhead base. The review will involve explaining variations from year to year and, in particular, will seek to identify any exceptional items as well as any ongoing changes to the overhead base.**

Such unofficial reports might contribute significantly to understanding the business and its current management (and the existence and use of such reports, of course, suggests that the management and control systems are open to improvement).

to the overhead base. The results of the review should indirectly give the clearest possible view on what the likely level of the overhead might be in the future.

The investigating accountant will draw on many sources of information in order to effect the review of the trading results. Typically he will begin with statutory and management accounting information, but he will also need to drill down to more detailed supporting information. He will particularly be interested in information which is used by the target's management to monitor and control the business. This information may not always be included in the official management accounting information, and there may be useful, and perhaps unofficial, reports kept in the 'top right-hand drawer' of key managers. Such unofficial reports might contribute significantly to understanding the business and its current management (and the existence and use of such reports, of course, suggests that the management and control systems are open to improvement).

As already discussed, the investigating accountant works a good deal through interviews. This is particularly important in the review of the trading results, where the investigating accountant will typically depend on a range of interviews in order to gain an understanding of the key forces driving the financial performance of the business.

Cash flow

During the course of the investigation the financial due diligence team will have learned much of how the operations of the business give rise to cashflows. It is valuable to pull this information together and to undertake any further research necessary to gaining a full understanding of the cash flows of the business.

In general, the investigating accountant will be aiming to understand the relationship between accounting profits and cash generation. A persistent failure to generate cash while continuing to show accounting profits might suggest that the profits, and the underlying accounting treatment, are questionable – the profits may not be real. A careful analysis of the items that reconcile profits to cash generation may highlight areas where the accounting treatment should be viewed with some suspicion.

The review will also seek to assess the quality of treasury management. Is the business financed efficiently? Does the management of the company have a full understanding of the cash flows of the business, such that movements in the cash position are predicted and managed in advance?

> **A persistent failure to generate cash while continuing to show accounting profits might suggest that the profits, and the underlying accounting treatment, are questionable – the profits may not be real.**

Case study – international shoe trade

In this case the review of trading results revealed a strong exposure to the dollar versus euro exchange rate. Unexpectedly, this was the source of a synergy between the business of the acquirer and the target.

The target was a manufacturer and distributor of shoes, based in northern Europe. The manufacturing part of the business had become very small, and the manufacture of almost all shoes was subcontracted to factories in the Far East and, to a small extent, in southern Europe. The target made almost all its sales in Europe, mainly in euros, with some sales in sterling. The acquirer had a similar business in North America.

The purchases of shoes in the Far East (for both the target and the acquirer) were necessarily made in US dollars. For the target therefore, an inherent long-term feature of the business was its exposure to the euro versus dollar exchange rate. Prior to the investigation, the euro had weakened against the dollar, significantly eroding the margins of the target. The target's customers were the major European retailers and management was failing in its attempts to pass on the effect of the weak euro in the form of increased selling prices.

The target could hedge against exchange rate movements in the relatively short term, covering a season's sales, for example, but it was not possible to take a long-term hedge to protect against exchange-rate movements.

The target business was therefore looking weaker than expected, and appeared extremely vulnerable to the euro versus dollar exchange rate. Further analysis and investigation, however, revealed a feature of the target

Case study – international shoe trade (continued)

which became interesting to the acquirer. With the weakening euro, the southern European shoe factories became more competitive suppliers to the target, and the margin on these products, of course, was not vulnerable to exchange-rate movements. The target was, therefore, effectively able to cap the exposure of its margin to the dollar versus euro exchange rate – below a certain value for the euro the southern European factories became cheaper than their competitors in the Far East, and any further decline in the euro did not matter.

Further investigation and analysis showed that not only could the southern European factories serve to protect the margins of the target, but also the North American acquirer could, through the target, access these factories. Below a certain dollar value for the euro these southern European factories allowed the acquirer to benefit from a weak euro and improve its own margins, and this on a business much bigger than that of the target. Hence, the due diligence investigation needed to be extended to assess the capacity of the European factories to supply the acquirer's needs. This kind of synergy was quite unhoped for before the acquirer commenced its due diligence investigation.

Case study – hosiery sales

The target was a French manufacturer of hosiery, and the acquirer had similar businesses in the UK. The review of the trading performance of the target revealed, or helped to understand in greater detail, some important features of the business:

- *Profits had declined over the last three years.* The major factor driving this downward trend turned out to be quite unusual, and not likely to be repeated regularly. The sales mix at the beginning of the period included very substantial sales of 'Fantasy' tights – heavily patterned tights, which were fashionable at the time. The target had spotted the new fashion before any of its competitors and took an unassailable lead on this part of the market. More sophisticated knitting machines were needed for Fantasy tights, and so the competition could not respond quickly to the new trend. The margins on Fantasy tights were particularly strong and drove the excellent overall performance of the target business. In the following two years the fashion for Fantasy tights gradually fell away, and this was the key reason behind the decline in the profits of the target. It became clear that, barring another one-off success such as the Fantasy product, the ongoing profitability of the target was better reflected by the lower profits of the latest year, rather than the high profits of three years previously.

- *The business of the target was quite strongly seasonal, with sales concentrated over the winter period.* This seasonality was considerably more marked than for the acquirer's business. The season began with the first cool weather of autumn. Sales for the year were vulnerable to the climate in the autumn and a prolonged summer simply resulted in a later start to the season, and a straight loss in sales that could not be caught up. In assessing the ongoing long-term profit trends, therefore, it was important to take into account when the season had begun compared with the long-term average.

- *There was a gradual increase in the competitive pressure from countries with lower labour costs, such as North Africa.* It was not clear that the target could depend only on its own factory in the long term, and it looked as though the production of the simpler products would need to be subcontracted to lower cost countries in due course. The financial investigation had revealed a decline in margins in respect of the lower value-added product lines, which appeared to reflect increasing pressure on prices due to the arrival on the market of producers with lower labour costs.

Case study – industrial sack manufacturer

In this case the target was part of a larger group and depended on the group for a range of services. To assess the ongoing profitability of the target, the review of the trading results needed to look carefully at the cost of the services provided by the group.

The target manufactured large industrial sacks used, for example, to package fertilizers. No other company in the group had an activity similar to that of the target.

The target was dependent on the group for certain centralized services, including:

- Accounting. The accounting software was run centrally by a centralized accounts team. The target had almost no accounting function of its own.

- Marketing. The group marketing department produced all the target's marketing material, although the target had its own dedicated sales force.

Case study – industrial sack manufacturer (continued)

The target had its own brand, but this appeared as secondary to the group's main brand in the marketing material.

- Insurance. The group insurance policy covered the target.

The group invoiced the target for these services. As part of the review of trading performance, the financial due diligence investigation looked at how these various group services would be provided by the acquirer following completion of the proposed acquisition. To a considerable extent it appeared that the acquirer would be able to provide these services without incurring any further costs; the existing resources of the acquirer looked to be able substantially to absorb the services that would be required by the target. So it looked as though the group charges invoiced to the target by the vendor could be reversed for the purposes of the acquirer's assessment of the target's likely contribution to earnings following completion of the proposed acquisition.

Net assets 14

A financial due diligence investigation of assets and liabilities does not constitute an audit of the assets and liabilities. Which is not to say that an audit may not be important, but the focus and objectives of an audit are quite different from those of a due diligence investigation. In a nutshell, an audit is primarily concerned with the past, whereas a due diligence investigation is concerned only with the future. An audit seeks to verify the existence, valuation (generally based on historical cost) and completeness of assets and liabilities; a due diligence review is concerned with the future capacity of a business to generate earnings, and the assets and liabilities of a business are of interest only insofar as they contribute to the future earnings potential of the business. Of course, this includes seeking to ascertain that all the assets and liabilities are appropriately recorded in the target's records, but it should also aim one step further: a financial due diligence review of assets and liabilitites should be driven by an assessment of the requirements of the business going forward.

In some ways the review of assets is inherently easier than that of liabilities. The nature of the assets renders them easier to find. The risk is that, for example, crucial assets may not be owned by the business. Liabilities are more difficult and it can be hard to find an undisclosed liability.

The review of assets, therefore, can rely extensively on the accounting records as a primary source of information, and as the starting point for enquiries. But the investigating accountant will seek to understand how a company's assets are used for the business. For example, whether the

> **An audit seeks to verify the existence, valuation (generally based on historical cost) and completeness of assets and liabilities; a due diligence review is concerned with the future capacity of a business to generate earnings.**

business has assets appropriate to its business, or whether the asset base is of appropriate quality, and is able to handle the volumes of business currently transacted, or forecast in the near future. There may be an urgent need to make substantial investments in new equipment, or there may be assets, perfectly valid from an accounting and audit point of view, which are not relevant to the core business. In which case an acquirer may be able to look at dispos-

> **The primary concern may well be with liabilities that do not figure in the accounting records. It will be important to make good use of soft information gained in interviews, and especially in interviews with employees far from finance (production or sales, for example), and perhaps quite junior employees less sensitive to the issues surrounding an acquisition.**

ing of some assets to realize cash and effectively reduce the consideration paid for the underlying business.

Similarly, the review of liabilities can begin with the accounting records. But the primary concern may well be with liabilities that do not figure in the accounting records. The investigating accountant cannot be sure of finding all unrecorded liabilities, but an experienced investigator will have a good idea of how to look. It will be important to make good use of soft information gained in interviews, and especially in interviews with employees far from finance (production or sales, for example), and perhaps quite junior employees less sensitive to the issues surrounding an acquisition. It will also be important to think laterally. For example, the customer who pays slowly, identified from a review for bad debts, may not simply represent a credit risk but may be the next source of a legal claim for damages for failure to perform a contract.

Examples of issues that might arise on a review of a company's assets and liabilities are as follows.

- A company might own the freehold of its main premises. But it may not be necessary to own these premises. An acquirer may like to consider entering into a sale and leaseback agreement which would release cash which might be a valuable resource following completion of an acquisition.

- Interviews with a production director might suggest that the production equipment of a business is outdated and is beginning to place the company at a competitive disadvantage. Equally, interviews with a production director should give a feel for capacity – and whether the current facility could take on significantly more work. There may be scope to develop synergies with an acquirer here.

- A review of fixed asset investments may reveal investments in non-core activities which could easily be disposed of without causing any harm to the mainstream business.

- A review of the terms of business may reveal that the target provides a generous warranty in respect of its products, but a review of the balance sheet may suggest that there is insufficient provision for the likely cost of such a warranty.
- A review of board minutes or minutes of more informal management meetings may reveal litigation for which no provision has been made in the accounts.

Case study – European new and second-hand goods retailer

In this case the financial investigation of a target revealed a substantial undisclosed liability to pay VAT.

The target was a retail chain, selling new and second-hand goods. The VAT regime applicable to the second-hand goods was different from that of the new goods: VAT was accounted for on the margin on second-hand good sales only.

The target's accounting records were poorly organized, with the result that the VAT accounting got out of control. At the same time the market turned against the target, with the result that the financial position of the target became weak.

The financial due diligence investigation came upon many VAT accounts, and was unable to obtain satisfactory explanations for these. Overall the balance sheet accounts seemed to suggest an unusually large liability to VAT, but clear information could not be obtained from the target. Accordingly the scope of the financial due diligence investigation was adjusted to incorporate a comprehensive VAT review, performed by an appropriate specialist.

A full VAT review revealed that there was indeed a large liability to VAT which had not been fully accounted for in the VAT returns. Moreover, the failure to account fully for the VAT in the returns exposed the target to very substantial penalties and interest.

The acquirer obtained appropriate warranties. But also, and with the agreement of the vendor, the acquirer disclosed the position fully to the VAT authorities immediately following completion of the transaction, and succeeded in agreeing a minimal level of penalties and interest.

Taxation **15**

t is fairly common practice for the financial due diligence team to undertake a general high level review of a target's taxation affairs. But the full tax investigation needs to be carried out by appropriate tax specialists. The financial due diligence team can prepare the tax review by obtaining general information on the tax affairs of the target, and by highlighting areas which appear likely to cause concern. For example, the financial due diligence team may obtain copies of recent tax declarations, may ascertain

> **The due diligence process will also seek to identify tax planning opportunities both within the target and associated with the acquisition itself.**

that the target is up to date with its taxation affairs, and may find out if there are any open disputes – or a history of dispute – with the tax authorities.

The due diligence process will also seek to identify tax planning opportunities both within the target and associated with the acquisition itself.

The following are examples of taxation issues that might be raised by the financial due diligence investigation:

- In a group context there may be trading among group companies, which may give rise to transfer pricing issues. This will be particularly true where there is intragroup trading across different tax jurisdictions where there is no possibility to form a tax consolidation.

- Similarly, within a group there may be taxation issues around any loan finance provided to or by the target and, again, this is more likely to be an issue where any loan finance is made across different tax jurisdictions.

- The tax treatment of any management fees will need to be reviewed with care, in particular where the fees are made across tax jurisdictions.

- Any tax credits arising on investments in research and development will need careful review, in order to assess the risk of such tax credits being brought into question.

- Tax losses will need to be carefully identified, and their potential future use to the acquirer will need to be assessed. The value of any tax losses can often be a tricky negotiating point on a transaction. For instance, the losses may be of no value to the

> **The value of any tax losses can often be a tricky negotiating point on a transaction.**

vendor, but of potential value to the acquirer. The vendor will of course seek to sell any such losses, but the acquirer may be reluctant to pay where there is no likely value to the vendor and where the value to the acquirer is necessarily uncertain.

- There may be potential to implement a creative tax structure. For example, in a transaction involving several tax jurisdictions it might be possible to implement a structure in which interest on loan finance is tax deductible twice or even three times. Where the target is financed by inter-company debt, the acquirer may be able to purchase the debt in a manner which is tax efficient for both the vendor and the acquirer.

> **In a transaction involving several tax jurisdictions it might be possible to implement a structure in which interest on loan finance is tax deductible twice or even three times.**

Case study – Spanish executive search*

The target was a Spanish subsidiary of an executive search group based in the UK. The UK group levied substantial management fees on the Spanish subsidiary, in the form of charges to cover use of the brand, general administration and commission on referred business.

In common with many other tax jurisdictions, the Spanish tax authorities tend to look closely at management fees charged to subsidiaries of international groups. The acquirer was concerned that a tax inspector would argue that the management fees were excessive and so not fully tax deductible in the hands of the Spanish subsidiary. This reasoning would expose the target to an additional tax assessment. The amounts involved were material in the context of the proposed transaction.

In this particular case the acquirer was not comfortable relying on a tax indemnity to provide protection against the perceived tax risk on the management fees, and this for two reasons:

1 The acquirer believed the risk of a tax reassessment to be high, and therefore believed that the proposed tax indemnity would be likely to be called (the vendor believed the risk to be low). Understandably the acquirer preferred to avoid putting in place an indemnity which it believed was likely to be called, not least because of the danger that the vendor might seek to dispute the claim, so draining management time and effort.

2 The vendor was not in a strong financial position and there was some concern that it might have difficulty in honouring the proposed tax indemnity.

Accordingly, it was agreed that the target business would be hived off into a new company, leaving the vendors with a corporate shell with which the tax risk remained. The acquirer then purchased the new company.

* This case study is only loosly based on the combined facts of two different real life deals, i.e. this case study should be treated as fiction.

Financial issues relating to Pension Schemes 16

The cost of pension benefits for staff and directors is often a significant element in a company's remuneration costs. A standard 'final salary' scheme may cost 20% or more on top of the total salaries bill but this cost may not be fully reflected in the current financial statements.

It is not always straightforward to identify what a company's true pension costs are what or they will be in the future. Salaries, overtime, bonuses, National Insurance contributions, other benefits (such as car, life assurance and medical cover) are known and largely controllable

Pension costs, may continue to be incurred many years into the future and long after the workforce for whom the pensions are provided has ceased to be employed.

and incurred at the same time as the services are received from staff. Pension costs, however, may continue to be incurred many years into the future and long after the workforce for whom the pensions are provided has ceased to be employed.

Over the years legislation governing pensions, including company pensions, has become increasingly complex and added significantly to this cost burden and the future uncertainty of the final costs.

Understanding the nature of the different types of pension arrangements in place for a company, and obtaining clear and up-to-date information on the future costs expected to be met by the company, are essential parts of the due diligence process.

This chapter should be read in conjunction with Chapter 27 which deals with pensions due diligence and explains the different types of pension scheme.

Of these, final salary schemes will naturally be of greater interest from the financial due diligence perspective and the remainder of this chapter relates to this type of scheme.

Final salary schemes

In the case of final salary schemes, actuarial valuations need to be carried out regularly in order to assess the value of the pension scheme assets and the present value of future pension payments to be able to determine the scheme's current solvency and the level of future contribution likely to be required.

Actuarial valuations

Legislation and practice has led to actuarial valuations being carried out for additional purposes and on different assumptions or bases. It is not uncommon therefore to find at any given date that a pension scheme has a surplus, or is overfunded, on one basis but is in deficit, or underfunded, on another.

It is not uncommon to find at any given date that a pension scheme has a surplus, or is overfunded, on one basis but is in deficit, or underfunded, on another.

Central to the understanding of the financial state of a final salary scheme, therefore, is an appreciation of the following different bases and the corresponding underlying purposes for which actuarial valuations may be carried out.

Funding

The traditional purpose of an actuarial valuation, to determine how the assets compare with the accumulated liability for past service pensions (resulting in current surplus or deficit) and the future rate of contribution required to meet future service benefits. The underlying assumptions are set by the scheme actuary based on past experience and his or her expectations for the future.

Minimum funding requirement (MFR)

Similar to the funding valuation, but on a method and assumptions closely prescribed by legislation and leading onto strict rules for payment of additional contributions by the company where deficits are calculated. The MFR has proved inflexible in changing financial conditions and for different scheme circumstances and is set to be replaced by a new standard by 2005.

Buy-out

If a pension scheme is wound up, the scheme benefits will usually be secured by buying out individual policies with an insurance company. The costs charged by insurance companies for buy-out policies are high relative to the costs assessed for an ongoing scheme.

FRS17

The pension costs shown in a company's accounts are calculated under a different set of rules, Financial Reporting Standard 17, which is being phased in over the period up to 22 June 2003, to replace the previous accounting standard, SSAP24. Under FRS17 companies will be required to recognize the value of a pension scheme deficit (and surplus to the extent recoverable by the company) in its balance sheet.

It follows from the above that there is considerable scope for disagreement between a buyer and seller of a business as to the net worth of the pension scheme as an asset or liability of that business. Specialist actuarial advice is therefore essential. The purchaser may need to commission its own independent calculations, so it is important that the question of pensions is flagged up as early as possible in the process. This is particularly relevant if the acquisition is of part of a business which requires an existing pension scheme to be split.

Other pensions issues

Other issues that may need to be addressed include:

- the existence of any unfunded pension promises to individual employees or directors;
- contingent liabilities arising from changes in legislation not currently allowed for;
- existing compliance with all aspects of pensions legislation and regulation;
- proposals for provision of past and future service pension benefits post-acquisition;
- transitional arrangements; and
- employment rights and expectations of target workforce.

Much of the information required for the due diligence investigation will be available from the following sources, but further enquiries may need to be made and additional data obtained in any particular case:

- trust deeds and rules for all schemes, including amendments;
- members' explanatory booklets and any announcements;
- annual trustees' reports and accounts for the scheme, latest and previous years;
- company accounts (pension scheme costs and disclosures); and
- actuarial valuation reports, latest and previous one, plus any related correspondence on actuarial position.

Financial projections 17

The entire due diligence investigation should, directly or indirectly, be concerned with improving the clarity with which the acquirer can look to the future performance of the target. The financial due diligence review should work towards building up a comprehensive understanding of the target and its business, and this will form a valuable base from which the investigating accountant can conduct his review of the financial projections.

Context of the projections

Not every financial due diligence investigation includes a review of financial projections. In some instances such a review may not be appropriate because, for example, the intention following the acquisition is to change substantially the circumstances of the target. In such cases, though, it may well be valuable to review the acquirer's business plan, including the financial projections, for the target. In some cases the target may simply not have prepared any financial projections or the projections may not have been prepared with sufficient thoroughness to make a proper review worthwhile.

> In some instances such a review may not be appropriate because, for example, the intention following the acquisition is to change substantially the circumstances of the target.

Structure of the projections

It is common for a financial due diligence investigation to be 'crowned' with a review of financial projections, to take the financial due diligence to its logical conclusion. Often the review of financial projections will fall into two parts.

1 There may be a review of an estimate or projection for the results to the end of the year in progress. Such an estimate will usually be based on management accounting information up until a recent date, together with any information on sales in the near future, based on orders, and with 'pure' forecast information to take the estimate up to the end of the year.

> Often the review of financial projections will fall into two parts.

Then there may be a review of the projected performance for one or two years following the year in progress.

2 Then there may be a review of the projected performance for one or two years following the year in progress.

Opinion given by investigating accountants

It is worth giving some thought to the nature of the opinion that investigating accountants will be prepared to give on the financial projections. For an acquirer it can be disappointing to read a review of projections only to find that the investigating accountant has merely described the projections without giving his view on their quality. Of course, an investigator cannot issue an opinion to the effect that the forecast will or will not be achieved. But the investigator can give comfort on the level of care that has gone into preparing the projections, and can make it clear whether he feels that the major assumptions

When instructing an investigating accountant it is important to discuss the strength of opinion that he will be prepared to give on the financial projections.

have been arrived at after appropriate research and in taking reasonable views on key future events outside the control of the target. When instructing an investigating accountant it is important to discuss the strength of opinion that he will be prepared to give on the financial projections.

Preparation of the projections

Prior to beginning the detailed review of projections the investigating accountant will be concerned to establish the circumstances in which the projections have been prepared, looking into issues such as the following.

The target's past experience of preparing forecast financial information

In many larger groups the budgeting process is key to the management of the business. Budgets are prepared in respect of each year as a matter of course, the actual performance against budget is closely monitored, and budgets may be revised, perhaps more than once, as the year progresses. In some owner-managed business there may be no formal budget, or the budget may simply be an objective for sales which is not then used in the management of the business.

In some owner-managed business there may be no formal budget, or the budget may simply be an objective for sales which is not then used in the management of the business.

Subsequent accuracy of any forecasts prepared in respect of past periods, including the current year

It may be that the target has always failed to meet its forecasts in the past, and this, of course, will suggest that the forecasts currently under review may not be achieved either.

The team which has been involved in preparing the forecast

It might be reassuring if the forecast has been prepared with heavy involvement of the operational management of the target, especially if it is this management team that will be responsible for achieving the forecast following completion of the proposed acquisition. On the other hand, it is often a cause for concern if a forecast has been prepared by a head office running the sale of the target, without the involvement of the local management. The investigator will wish to see the forecasts formally approved and adopted by appropriate managers, perhaps from a head office and, more importantly, from the operational management of the target.

Earnouts

Where an earnout has been negotiated, it is worth taking care to understand the motivation of those involved in the preparation of the forecasts. For instance, a vendor may even be inclined to understate likely future performance since this might allow the vendor to negotiate an earnout which he expects to achieve with ease. Or, a management team that is not directly interested in the sale proceeds, but more interested in getting off to a good start with the new owners, may be inclined to understate likely future performance in order to set easily achievable targets.

In general

By becoming familiar with the circumstances in which the projections have been prepared, the investigating accountant will be able to form an initial view on the quality of projections which the target is capable of preparing.

Moreover, and especially in respect of a business for sale, it is common for forecasts to show a significant improvement in the performance of the business compared with that currently being achieved. In conducting the review the investigating accountant will seek to test the forecast, in order to identify where its weaknesses lie.

Link with commercial due diligence

Commercial due diligence tends to be strongly focused on future movements in markets and, in particular, on how the target might fare on those markets; this work will typically help point to the level of sales that might be achieved by the target in the future. And it is on the question of future sales that the investigating accountant feels most vulnerable – he may be able to use much of his investigation to give some comfort on the level of margins and overheads, but may well have gained only limited comfort on future sales. So this is an instance where close communication between the commercial due diligence and the financial due diligence teams can be invaluable.

It is on the question of future sales that the investigating accountant feels most vulnerable – this is an instance where close communication between the commercial due diligence and the financial due diligence teams can be invaluable.

The review of the forecasts

The following are other ways in which the investigating accountant will seek to gain comfort on the forecasts.

Careful analysis of past performance compared with the forecast

The direction of the investigation will be driven by the need to underpin any strong movements shown in the forecast. The investigator will also wish to look at any failure of the forecast to show expected movements. For example, the investigator may be expecting a decline in gross margin because there may recently have been a significant increase in the cost of raw materials, but the forecast may show an improvement in gross margin.

The investigation will be looking for as much solid supporting evidence of sales as possible

If the forecast shows a price increase, it will be interesting to see to what extent the price increase has already been agreed with customers. If it is not agreed, it will be worth looking at the past success of introducing price increases, and it may be worth looking into the pricing policies of competitors. Here again the commercial due diligence team will be able to help. Detailed analyses of forecast sales will be needed – by product, by customer and perhaps by supplier. This will enable the investigator to see where growth is to come from, and then to focus subsequent investigations into assessing the credibility of that growth.

Regarding margins the investigation will look into selling prices, purchase prices and production costs

It will be useful to understand where the power lies in the target's relationship with its suppliers – which is more dependent on the other, and so who is in the driving seat. Also, for example, whether the factory has the capacity to meet the forecast growth – it will be important to understand where the bottlenecks in the production process lie, since these will be the key constraints on capacity. Here it will be necessary to look at production records and to discuss these with those responsible for production. If there are to be improvements in productivity, it will be important to understand how they are to be achieved. Production records may already show evidence of productivity improvements which have not yet fed through to an improvement in accounting margins.

> **It will be useful to understand where the power lies in the target's relationship with its suppliers – which is more dependent on the other, and so who is in the driving seat.**

The investigation will include a detailed review of the forecast overheads compared to historical overheads

Other things being equal, one may well expect overheads to be stable, with perhaps a small increase for inflation. It will be important to establish which costs are fixed and which are variable, and for variable costs it will be necessary to understand what are the key drivers. It will be worth seeing whether the forecast includes some sort of contingency for unforeseen costs. Quite apart from the need (or not) for a contingency, the existence of a contingency and its size may say something about the aims of those responsible for the forecast. For instance, there may be an attempt to deflate forecast results which may also exist elsewhere in the forecast but less visibly.

Synergies on the acquisition

It is common for forecasts to be prepared on a stand-alone basis, as if the target were to continue trading in its current environment, without taking into account the impact of a planned acquisition. In this case the investigating accountant may seek to identify, and perhaps quantify, any obvious synergies arising on a purchase of the target by the acquirer. In some cases the acquirer and the target may work together in order to incorporate synergies into the forecast, and the financial due diligence may include a review of these forecast synergies, and the costs of their implementation.

It is common for forecasts to be prepared on a stand-alone basis, as if the target were to continue trading in its current environment, without taking into account the impact of a planned acquisition.

International issues **18**

I n many respects a financial due diligence investigation should be conducted in the same manner regardless of the jurisdiction of the companies concerned. However, different countries have very different attitudes towards
due diligence, and this can have a considerable effect on the nature and scope
of an investigation.

Business practice and culture

For example, in some countries it is not usual to conduct an extensive pre-
acquisition investigation. This may simply be a matter of local business practice, but there may also be a legal basis for such differences. For example, the
UK concept of *caveat emptor,* of course, is not applicable across the world.
Equally, to initiate the due diligence process in the UK one is used to seeing a
letter of intent or similar document in place, and this provides the legal framework within which the due diligence investigations can be conducted. In a
jurisdiction where it is difficult to achieve a non-binding letter of intent, it
is difficult to open up a period of pre-
acquisition due diligence at all – once
the buyer is legally committed to the
deal, any investigation work is not
really 'pre-acquisition' at all.

Issues of culture and business
practice become important in cross-
border transactions. The interests of a
buyer and seller are fundamentally
opposed in many ways. With respect to
due diligence, it is in the interest of the

**In some countries it is not
usual to conduct an
extensive pre-acquisition
investigation. This may
simply be a matter of local
business practice, but
there may also be a legal
basis for such differences.**

buyer to effect thorough investigations of the target before comitting to a
deal. But this is dangerous for the seller who may in the course of the due
diligence give away highly sensitive competitive information to a prospective
buyer – who may then withdraw from the process and use that information
to improve his own business at the expense of the target. The target's interests are best served if the purchaser is bound prior to having access to any
sensitive information.

This conflict of interest between buyer and seller is resolved differently in different countries' usual business practice. For example, in the UK the usual practice is relatively favourable to buyers: it is usual for buyers to effect substantial investigations prior to becoming bound to complete a deal. On the European continent, the standard practice often resolves this conflict more in favour of the seller, and it is usual for buyers to commit to a transaction without effecting such detailed investigations of the target.

As a result, cross-border transactions can generate particular tensions and misunderstandings. Imagine the case of a UK buyer of a French target. The UK buyer is used to carrying out detailed investigations of a target before becoming committed to a transaction. The French seller is used to selling without giving extensive access to confidential information on the target. So when the French seller declines to allow the UK buyer access to the target company's records, the UK buyer naturally begins to imagine that there must be something to hide, and that it must be bad, so the buyer loses confidence. But the French seller may react badly to the UK purchaser's demands: from the seller's point of view, it is not normal to ask to conduct such a detailed investigation, and he begins to suspect that the UK buyer is not really a buyer at all but someone trying to mount an operation of industrial espionage. So trust can very easily break down – a poor environment for conducting a deal, to say the least!

> **In the UK the usual practice is relatively favourable to buyers: it is usual for buyers to effect substantial investigations prior to becoming bound to complete a deal.**

The solution? Put these issues on the table right at the start. Be ready for culture and business practice to differ from country to country. Once it is clearly understood where each party is coming from, and it is clear that no one is acting in bad faith, it is merely a matter of agreeing on some sort of compromise procedure. In an environment of mutual trust and respect this is not insurmountable.

> **Once it is clearly understood where each party is coming from, and it is clear that no one is acting in bad faith, it is merely a matter of agreeing on some sort of compromise procedure.**

Financial due diligence is particularly vulnerable to these issues of culture and business practice. This is because effective financial due diligence depends a great deal on the investigating accountant having extensive access to the target company and its key managers and staff.

Commercial due diligence can often raise fewer difficulties because the main investigation work is carried out away from the target company. In fact, there is not much a target could do to limit the investigation and the target may not even know much about the commercial investigation.

Legal due diligence relies a great deal on documents and less on interviews than financial due diligence. This can be sensitive for targets, but often it seems easier for a target to disclose documents than to allow prolonged access to the target business and its key managers. It is also perhaps fair to say that gaps in legal due diligence can more easily be flushed out through disclosures and warranties than can gaps in financial due diligence.

Other general cross-border issues

There are some further general ways in which the conduct of a financial due diligence investigation varies according to the country of the target.

- The ease with which access to the working papers of auditors will be granted. In the UK and the USA auditors tend to be reluctant to grant access to their working papers. In other countries the auditors may open up their files much more easily.

- The quality of management information may tend to vary country by country. It may be fair to say that the best quality management information tends to be found in the Anglo-Saxon countries or in companies or groups with an Anglo-Saxon style of management – although here there can be a tendency to produce very large volumes of information without necessarily giving careful thought to what information is most pertinent to measuring the underlying performance of the business. In some countries it is not standard practice to produce monthly management accounts, and even annual statutory accounts may not be produced until well after the year end.

- Similar considerations apply to the preparation and use of business plans, budgets and forecast financial information.

> **In some countries it is not standard practice to produce monthly management accounts, and even annual statutory accounts may not be produced until well after the year end.**

Specific technical issues

Often cited, but usually relatively easy to resolve, are the technical differences found in various jurisdictions. For the purposes of financial due diligence these are not usually a major feature of cross-border transactions: the technical differences are not too difficult for the appropriate experts to pin down and assess. The more important issues which can arise quite often include the following.

- The definition of financial debt. Old favourites here are leases and debt supported by working capital assets. Certain kinds of lease may be treated as simple rental contracts in one country, but treated as though the underlying asset had been purchased and financed by a loan in another country. Similarly, some invoice discounting transactions are accounted for off the balance sheet in some countries, but give rise to financial debt on the balance sheet in other countries. These definitions can be key in instances where the price of a company has been negotiated debt free.

- Provisions for pensions and similar liabilities. Some kinds of pension commitment will not be provided for in certain countries, but would be provided for under the accounting rules of other countries.

- The accounting treatment of goodwill, and particularly goodwill arising on consolidation, varies across different countries.

Certain kinds of lease may be treated as simple rental contracts in one country, but treated as though the underlying asset had been purchased and financed by a loan in another country.

But, when assessing the financial strength of a business, and its potential to generate profits in the future, pure technical issues such as these are not key. The heart of a financial investigation, therefore, remains constant across jurisdictions. It is the implementation of the investigation that can be difficult to achieve in some countries.

Cross-border integration issues

Cross-border transactions raise particular issues for the post-acquisition integration of the target. The financial investigation should seek to anticipate these issues, assessing the current abilities of the target's management compared to the likely requirements following completion of the acquisition.

It is common for a new subsidiary in another country to need to review its financial reporting and control structures, often for two main reasons.

1 A foreign owner will perhaps be especially concerned to put tight financial controls in place. Such an owner may feel that the subsidiary is 'far away', and, in another culture, inherently less easy to control and master. No chances can be taken therefore with weak financial controls.

2 The subsidiary will no doubt be required to report its performance in accordance with the requirements of its new owner, using a particular reporting style and format, and applying the owner's accounting policies.

Equally, post-acquisition it will be important to establish and maintain good ongoing communication between the owner's and the subsidiary's management teams. Often this can be achieved if one of the subsidiary's managers is particularly comfortable with the holding company management – from the same country, for example, but also well integrated into the subsidiary's local culture. This role can often be filled by the subsidiary's finance director, perhaps the subsidiary's second most senior manager, and the issues of financial reporting and control can thus be tackled at the same time.

Applying the results **19**

The results of a financial due diligence investigation will need to be acted upon. Various kinds of action may be appropriate; it will depend on the nature of the findings of the investigation.

The acquisition strategy

If the results of the investigation fail to support the original acquisition strategy, it may be appropriate to abandon the transaction altogether. Or it may be possible to revise the strategy in the light of the new information. In an ideal world, it should only be issues of strategy that lead to a transaction failing to complete; other issues arising on due diligence, but with no impact on the acquisition strategy, should be possible to manage through the negotiations for the acquisition.

For example, the strategy driving an acquisition may be the understanding that the target company has cheaper manufacturing costs for a product than the equivalent manufacturing costs of the prospective acquiring company. A well-planned financial investigation would look closely at the manufacturing costs of the target, compared with those of the prospective purchaser. Should it appear that the target's manufacturing costs are greater than initially thought, the acquisition strategy would be undermined, and so it may well be appropriate to withdraw from the acquisition process.

Price negotiation

It is not unusual for the results of financial due diligence to lead to a renegotiation of the price.

Earnouts

The financial due diligence process may raise questions over the ongoing profitability of the target, and this may lead to a renegotiation of the price. There may be disagreement between the parties on the potential for future profits, and this may be resolved by agreeing upon a price which is dependent on the level of future profits (an earnout).

Vendors will want to control profitability in the earnout period, and this may result in fundamental conflicts with the new owners.

To agree upon earnout consideration may often provide a satisfactory resolution to a disagreement over the level of future profits. But earnouts can raise a number of problems which can be difficult to resolve and which can hamper progress with the integration of the newly acquired company following completion of the acquisition. Worth careful thought in the context of an earnout will be:

- How the target is to be controlled during the earnout period. The business will have new owners who will want to exercise control and will be focused on achieving seamless integration into the acquirer's businesses. But the vendors will want to control profitability in the earnout period, and this may result in fundamental conflicts with the new owners. The conflictual environment so created may hamper integration, even afer the earnout is over.

- Under an earnout the vendors may become highly focused on short-term profitability, at the expense of longer-term prospects, and lose sight of an interest in longer-term strategy. Following the earnout period it may prove difficult to recapture focus on longer-term strategy.

- Following the acquisition it is inevitable that the new ownership will have some impact on the business. In which case it may become difficult to measure the profits to which an earnout is to be applied. For example, there may be disagreements on the treatment of business brought to the target by the new owners, especially if such new business is not profitable in the target, although it may be in the wider interests of the group.

- Treatment of the earnout if one or more vendors/managers leaves the business before the end of the earnout period. The acquirer may be reluctant to pay an earnout in such circumstances, but if the earnout is not payable when a vendor leaves, the vendor will be concerned that the acquirer might deliberately seek to provoke his departure in order to avoid paying the earnout.

Earnouts can work well. But their negotiation is often complex and can be fraught. The financial due diligence investigation should help to assess how appropriate an earnout might be for a given transaction. For example it will be necessary to take into account the quality of profits, the level of dependence on the vendors to achieve profits and, perhaps of most importance, the integration plans post-acquisition.

There may be disagreements on the treatment of business brought to the target by the new owners.

Price agreed free of debt and cash

It is common practice to negotiate a valuation of a business free of financial debt and cash. Which is clear and simple in principle. In practice it can be difficult to define what is meant by financial debt and cash. These difficulties are heightened in the case of cross-border transactions: what is considered to be financial debt in one country may not be disclosed as such in another country.

It will be necessary to give careful thought to the meaning of cash and debt, which may bring to light a disagreement between the vendor and the acquirer.

Where a valuation free of financial debt and cash has been agreed upon, the financial due diligence should seek to assess the likely level of net debt, or cash, at completion. As part of this process it will be necessary to give careful thought to the meaning of cash and debt, which may bring to light a disagreement between the vendor and the acquirer. It may then become necessary to re-open the price negotiations.

A particular difficulty arises in the case of a seasonal business. Where the business is seasonal, the level of cash or debt will also be seasonal. So what is to be done if completion occurs at a time when the business is particularly cash rich? Just after Christmas in the case of a high street retailer, for example? To effect the transaction with a price adjustment for the net cash position at completion would be to favour the vendor – the acquirer will acquire a business with a peak in its cash position, but the cash is not truly free cash since it will disappear as the business moves through its annual cycle. In such cases it is common to seek to ascertain the average working capital requirement of the business, and to measure the level of financial debt or cash at completion after adjusting to take account of any seasonal variation in the working capital requirement.

It is common to seek to ascertain the average working capital requirement of the business, and to measure the level of financial debt or cash at completion after adjusting to take account of any seasonal variation in the working capital requirement.

This part of the price clause in the sale and purchase agreement should be drafted in the light of what the financial due diligence investigation has revealed of the seasonal movements in the working capital requirement; the

Unlike much of the sale and purchase agreement, these clauses will be closely read and implemented after completion

lawyers and accountants will need to work closely together on what will become a complex set of clauses, tricky to draft and negotiate, and tough to implement. Unlike much of the sale and purchase agreement, these clauses will necessarily be closely read and implemented after completion, even if the transaction proceeds smoothly and with no warranty claims.

Negotiation of declarations and warranties

Financial due diligence is likely to reveal some undisclosed liabilities, and contingent liabilities, as well as overstated assets. This often is not a reflection on the good faith or otherwise of the vendors. The vendors may themselves not be aware of all the possible liabilities of the business.

The financial due diligence team should review the declarations and warranties incorporated into the sale and purchase agreement, and should assess the extent to which the declarations and warranties provide protection against undisclosed liabilities or overvalued assets. Here it will again be particularly important that the legal and financial due diligence teams work closely together. The financial due diligence team will need carefully to explain the nature of the risks it perceives, and the legal team will then need to assess how best to obtain suitable protection in the documentation.

The vendors may themselves not be aware of all the possible liabilities of the business.

Structuring

The findings of the financial due diligence are likely to have an impact on the structure which is adopted for the acquisition.

• If the financial due diligence reveals many liabilities of an uncertain nature, it may be that the acquirer would wish to leave those liabilities unambiguously with the vendor. This may be achievable by making an acquisition of the business and its assets, rather than of the corporate vehicle which owns the business and its assets. But this will depend on the jurisdiction – there may be unfavourable tax effects of an asset deal.

- On the other hand, if financial due diligence confirms that a target has a high level of tax losses brought forward, the acquirer may very much wish to purchase the corporate vehicle in order to acquire the tax losses.

- It may be possible to leave debt in the target company in order to generate tax deductible interest charges. This might be achieved pre-acquisition by agreeing with a vendor group that the target should be sold with a certain amount of financial debt to be taken over by the purchaser, the purchase consideration to be reduced by an equivalent amount. This can be achieved, for example, by the vendors causing the target to take out new loans, the cash thus raised being paid out to the vendors pre-acquisition. The results of the financial due diligence investigations will help to establish the best manner in which the target can be delivered with the requisit amount of debt.

- The financial due diligence investigation may help establish the best means of paying up future profits to the new purchaser. For example, the investigation may establish that the top company of the target has no distributable reserves, such that dividends may not be paid in the near term, and so other means of paying up profits need to be put in place. It is usually advantageous to identify any such constraints pre-acquisition, because an elegant solution may only be open pre-acquisition or may impact on the manner in which the acquisition itself is effected.

- The investigation may identify key managers whom the purchaser would want to tie into the business, and it may be appropriate to take this into account in structuring the acquisition, perhaps by leaving a minority shareholding with such key managers. It may be most efficient to effect this kind of transaction as part of the acquisition itself rather than as a subsequent and separate transaction.

Post-acquisition integration

The financial due diligence investigation should be keeping an eye on post-acquisition integration issues. Following completion of an acquisition a buyer will want to deal with any pressing integration issues as a matter of priority. So, of course, it should help matters if the due diligence investigations can identify integration issues early on. Integration issues frequently identified by the financial investigation include the following:

- In the case of an entrepreneurial owner-managed business, the financial direction of the target may be weak. The importance of any such weaknesses may be greater in the case of cross-border transactions. As part of the financial due diligence review it should be possible to assess the strength of the financial direction of the target, and to propose how any pressing improvements might be made. For example, it may be appropriate to instruct a headhunter to recruit a new finance director, even before the transaction is completed.

- There may be differences in the accounting policies adopted by the target and the acquirer. Following completion of the deal it will be necessary to bring the target's accounting policies into line with those of the new parent, at least for the purposes of monthly management accounts.

- Due diligence might reveal that the target has a major supplier in common with the acquirer. Following completion of the acquisition there may be scope to improve terms with that supplier – as a minimum one would aim to align the terms of both the target and the acquirer.

PART 3
Legal due diligence

Undertaking legal due diligence **20**

Why undertake legal due diligence?

This chapter considers the topic of legal due diligence from two angles: the process of legal due diligence and the general legal issues relating to a due diligence programme.

A common reaction amongst purchasers when considering the value of legal due diligence is: 'won't it just cost a lot, delay the transaction and tell me what I already know?' In some cases this is possibly true; not all due diligence investigations uncover something untoward. However, there are some strong arguments in favour of a legal due diligence programme.

Prior knowledge is better than litigation

It is perfectly possible for a purchaser to buy a company just relying on warranties and indemnities and what the seller is prepared to disclose to the purchaser against the warranties in the formal disclosure letter. However, if things go wrong, the seller has the money and the buyer faces bringing a court action for a remedy should the seller not agree to meet the claim. Litigation is costly and time consuming and there can be many obstacles to a successful claim (for instance, an individual seller may have relocated abroad together with his assets). Moreover, even if the purchaser is successful with his claim and obtains an order for costs to be met by the seller, it is a rule of thumb that the purchaser is only likely to recover approximately 70 to 75% of his costs on assessment (the court process whereby the reasonableness of costs is determined) although indemnity costs can be awarded by the court in special circumstances, for example where the other party has behaved unreasonably. The purchaser is therefore often likely to be out of pocket. Consequently, it is preferable to try and identify problems before buying a company rather than relying on warranty and indemnity claims afterwards. Furthermore, prior identification of problems can help identify 'deal breakers' early and also the correct price to pay. It is not unknown for due diligence to lead directly to a price renegotiation.

Discovery of attempts by the seller wilfully to conceal information

Wilful concealment of material information (or fraud, if one prefers to be more direct about it) is often difficult to discover if the seller is determined to hide the information. However, one thing is certain: just relying on warranties and indemnities without further investigation is unlikely to uncover fraud or other wrongdoing, whereas legal and financial due diligence can sometimes identify suspicious activity.

Discovery of previously unidentified problems

The greater probability, however, is that the seller is honest. Experience suggests that most sellers are so concerned about warranty and indemnity liability that they give painstaking attention to the detail of the warranties and the disclosure process. What are much more likely to come to light are previously unidentified problems. Not every company engages professionals to review every aspect of its business and while a seller may genuinely believe that his company is problem-free and clean, a due diligence programme can sometimes uncover difficulties which had not been identified previously. Professional advice can be expensive and this is relatively so in the early years of the development of a company. Decisions may be taken in ignorance of their full legal ramifications. It is often not that the seller is being in any way dishonest or attempting to mislead the purchaser, but that he genuinely does not have the necessary professional skills to spot the problem. For a purchaser paying a full price, however, an investment in a thorough due diligence programme prior to the acquisition will help to spot previously unidentified problems.

> Experience suggests that most sellers are so concerned about warranty and indemnity liability that they give painstaking attention to the detail of the warranties and the disclosure process.

Identification of necessary consents and releases

The increasing complexity of the law and business relationships means that there is a tendency for the sale of a company or business to require certain consents or releases. These can be manyfold. For instance, a release of the target company's shares from a parent company debenture, clearances from merger control authorities, approvals from significant suppliers or customers and releases or roll-over of employees' share options. Some of these matters may not be immediately apparent both to the purchaser and seller and thus the legal advisers can help identify the requisite steps to be taken in good time so that they do not unduly delay the transaction.

The parties should recognize that most of the due diligence information will form the foundation for legal liability in connection with the sale of a company or business. Invariably, the information resulting from a due diligence programme will be collected and collated and will find its way into the disclosure letter. This suits the seller because the contents of the disclosure letter will qualify the warranties in the sale agreement and exempt the seller from warranty liability for the matters disclosed. It also benefits the purchaser because the contents of the disclosure letter, including the due diligence information, will normally be the subject of warranties under the sale agreement.

Can the purchaser undertake due diligence itself?

To an extent every purchaser undertakes some due diligence itself. The key question is whether the purchaser should instruct professionals to carry out all or any part of the formal investigations. The advantages of instructing a legal adviser include the following.

Expert knowledge

As mentioned above, the purchaser and seller may simply not understand that a problem exists. An adviser with the requisite knowledge will be able to identify such problems and, hopefully, make suggestions on how to resolve them.

Resources

An acquisition is a time-consuming exercise for both the seller and purchaser and the purchaser may simply not have the manpower to conduct the due diligence himself. Drafting in outside professionals will ease the burden on the purchaser and leave it to concentrate on essentially commercial issues (including making effective commercial and risk management judgements about the information uncovered).

Insurance

Not only does this refer to the legal adviser's professional indemnity insurance, but also to the comfort of knowing that a professional has investigated the target company's affairs.

Political considerations

Professional advisers are usually untainted by the politics of the purchaser's organization and how the internal balance of power may be affected by a

There should be clear demarcation of each adviser's responsibilities with one adviser appointed to co-ordinate the due diligence programme (ideally the adviser who is closest to the commercial negotiations).

certain acquisition. Delivery of bad news is therefore often easier politically for an outside adviser than it may be for an employee reporting to a board of directors which might favour the proposed transaction. Whilst an employee's opinions can easily be dismissed as representing a negative attitude, this is more difficult with outside advisers.

The lawyer's relations with other advisers

In any due diligence process the legal adviser, once engaged, should, as a first step, brief himself about which other professionals he will be working with and the ambit of their investigations. There should be clear demarcation of each adviser's responsibilities with one adviser appointed to co-ordinate the due diligence programme (ideally the adviser who is closest to the commercial negotiations).

The legal adviser should also enquire about any due diligence which the purchaser will be undertaking. This is perhaps obvious guidance, but the purchaser will want to avoid the professionals tripping over each other, duplicating work and costs and unnecessarily irritating the seller with requests for similar information.

Where other advisers have completed their due diligence programmes in advance of the legal due diligence (perhaps because, as in the case of financial or environmental due diligence, the lead times involved in preparing reports tend to be longer), the legal adviser should be forewarned of areas which merit special attention. This will be of great assistance to the legal adviser not only in undertaking his own due diligence but also in drafting the legal documentation. A well organized purchaser will ensure that all points of concern are communicated to the legal advisers.

Is due diligence required legally?

The short answer is no. However, corporate governance guidelines recommend that significant acquisitions should be reserved to the full board of directors of the purchasing company. To ensure that the board considers all the issues, due diligence reports may be required. It is recommended that non-executive directors could play a key role in this respect by acting in a devil's advocate role. It is, however, difficult to see how they could fulfil this role without having independent reports from professional advisers on which to base their views – otherwise they would be dependent on the executive management.

Listed companies are bound by the Listing Rules of the UK Listing Authority (part of the Financial Services Authority). Where the acquisition by a listed company is a major one in relation to its group, requiring the approval of its shareholders, then a financial report on the merged group will be required. This makes a detailed accountants' investigation a prerequisite for the preparation of the circular to the purchaser's own shareholders.

> **Corporate governance guidelines recommend that significant acquisitions should be referred to the full board of directors of the purchasing company. To ensure that the board considers all the issues, due diligence reports may be required.**

Case study – Atlantic Computers

The purchaser

British & Commonwealth Holdings plc (B&C) acquired Atlantic Computers plc and its worldwide subsidiaries (Atlantic) for £408 million in September 1988.

During the mid-1980s B&C underwent a rapid transformation from a broadly based industrial group to a diversified financial services group largely as a result of acquisitions and disposals. As a result of this rapid restructuring, B&C had evolved a distinctive 'hands-off' management approach, with each subsidiary division of B&C expected to manage itself with minimum head office interference. This approach entailed placing a high degree of trust in the competence and integrity of those running the subsidiary divisions. The B&C board had only two non-executive directors and was comprised mainly of divisional heads. In practice, most authority rested with the chairman, the chief executive and the finance director.

The seller

Despite rapid growth in the 1970s and 1980s, Atlantic's principal business was and remained until its demise in 1990 that of computer leasing. Atlantic conducted most of its business by means of an arrangement known as a

Case study – Atlantic Computers (continued)

'Flexlease', which usually comprised two documents: a lease agreement and a management agreement.

Lease agreement

Typically this had a six-year term and was made between the end-user and the funder (who normally had acquired from Atlantic the equipment and the benefit of the lease agreement which Atlantic had in most cases arranged).

Management agreement

This was made between Atlantic and the end-user who had the benefit of the following options:

- the Flex option: this allowed the end-user to enter into a new lease for different equipment after three years;
- the Walk option: this allowed the end-user to terminate the lease after five years.

Under the management agreement Atlantic agreed to meet the end-user's obligations to the funder under the lease in the event that the end-user exercised the Flex and the Walk options. The Flexlease, therefore, gave rise to large potential liabilities to Atlantic which in practice were unlikely to be wholly offset by the residual resale value of the leased computer equipment.

Due diligence and the role of the professional advisers

The fatal flaw, as a DTI report subsequently concluded, was the failure of B&C and its professional advisers to adopt a 'thorough professional approach to its professional enquiries', particularly in relation to Atlantic's single product, the Flexlease. By giving the end-user the best of all worlds (i.e. the benefit of lower rentals associated with a long finance lease with the option to change its computer equipment before the end of the lease in order to keep up with technological advances), Atlantic had assumed large potential liabilities under these arrangements – much of which B&C, after a realistic assessment of residual risks, should have realized were likely to materialize in the long term.

The DTI report, in particular, highlighted the following shortcomings in B&C's due diligence programme:

- Despite dealing with a willing seller, B&C was insufficiently robust in its enquiries and did not press home its questions when it met resistance or received unsatisfactory answers.

- B&C accepted written answers to its questions which it should have recognized were unsatisfactory or incomplete.

- B&C did not obtain either a professional legal analysis of the Flexlease or professional advice concerning Atlantic's inappropriate accounting policies.

- Despite being advised by one of its advisers (see OC&C below) on the impossibility of assessing Atlantic's residual risks on the basis of publicly available information alone, B&C accepted without supporting evidence the misleading assertion of the Atlantic directors that it had no residual risks of any significance.

- B&C's relationships with its professional advisers – the merchant bank Barclays de Zoete Wedd (BZW) and a firm of strategy consultants, Outram Cullinan & Co. Ltd (OC&C) – were ill-defined, in particular:

  - BZW. BZW did not receive formal written instructions defining its role in the acquisition. Although B&C told the DTI inspectors that it was looking to BZW to assist and advise in the evaluation of Atlantic's business and its suitability for acquisition, BZW described its role as one of co-ordinating and facilitating, and not advising on, the commercial merits of the acquisition.

  - OC&C. OC&C Ltd was engaged to conduct an independent investigation into Atlantic and the computer leasing industry. There was a conflict of evidence as to whether B&C or BZW was OC&C's client. The DTI inspectors concluded that the resulting confusion over roles and reporting lines was a factor contributing towards B&C's failure to gain an adequate understanding of Atlantic's business prior to the takeover. Although OC&C expressed reservations about the high-risk nature of the computer leasing industry in general and Atlantic's residual risks under the Flexlease in particular, OC&C Ltd was not effective in following through with or driving home to the B&C board its doubts about the acquisition.

Case study – Atlantic Computers (continued)

The lessons

In terms of legal due diligence two key lessons can be drawn from this unfortunate acquisition.

1 *Role of professional advisers.* This should be clearly defined at the outset of any transaction in the form of a letter of engagement, which should be amended if the role of the professional adviser changes during the course of a transaction. As mentioned earlier, BZW operated without a letter of engagement which, although not uncommon with investment banks in the late 1980s, is less likely to be the case today.

2 *Role of the purchaser's board of directors.* Although it is invariably necessary to delegate the responsibility for the conduct of a due diligence programme to key directors, significant acquisitions should not proceed without the full board of directors having the information (including the doubts of any professional advisers) and the opportunity to consider independently the merits of the transaction. The DTI was told by several of B&C's divisional heads that the board meeting to approve the Atlantic acquisition was to a large extent a 'rubber-stamping' exercise. Following the introduction of corporate governance rules companies are more likely to have strong, independent board representation to whom the unpopular but necessary role of devil's advocate may be assigned.

The legal due diligence **21** process

How is LDD conducted?

There are several ways of undertaking legal due diligence.

Site visits

The most obvious way is for representatives of the purchaser and/or its advisers personally to visit the premises of the target company. However, if confidentiality is a key issue this might prove difficult, with the degree of access dependent upon the co-operation of the seller and the top management of the target company. If access is given to the target company's top management, these managers may prove more willing than the sellers to disclose matters to the purchaser unless the rationale for the purchase is known to involve the wholesale removal of the target company's top management. For this reason sellers may try to restrict access to continuing management.

Questionnaire/preliminary enquiries

Detailed written questions can be posed, to which the seller and his advisers will be asked to respond. As a practical tip, it is essential to keep a careful record of all information provided, when and to whom. This should be dealt with through a central point in order to avoid duplication and confusion.

Data rooms

If there is a number of potential purchasers, the seller may put together a data room where financial and commercial information about the target business is collected together for all potential purchasers to review. The objective will be to give potential purchasers sufficient information to enable them to put in indicative bids for the target company.

> As a practical tip, it is essential to keep a careful record of all information provided, when and to whom. This should be dealt with through a central point in order to avoid duplication and confusion.

> **Even if there is only one potential purchaser, sometimes the seller will put together information bundles for the purchaser in order to speed up the due diligence process.**

Once these bids have been assessed, the preferred bidder will usually be allowed to conduct a normal due diligence programme afterwards.

Seller's due diligence

Even if there is only one potential purchaser, sometimes the seller will put together information bundles for the purchaser in order to speed up the due diligence process. This is sometimes known as seller's due diligence. While this can be very helpful, such information is often supplemented by responses to specific questions raised by the purchaser. Another form of seller due diligence occurs where the seller arranges for his accountants to conduct an investigation into the affairs of the target company and to prepare a report which can be shown to a potential purchaser. The purchaser will wish to establish at the outset whether the report will be addressed to the purchaser personally to be able to place legal reliance upon it. If so, it will significantly enhance the usefulness of such a report. It may be considered even more useful if it is prepared by independent accountants as a special exercise for the purpose.

Disclosure letter

It should not be forgotten that the disclosure letter itself is a source of due diligence information. It is not just the final version of the disclosure letter which is submitted to the purchaser during the sale negotiations. It invariably goes through a succession of drafts. Each draft will disclose more information and the purchaser and its advisers will invariably ask questions about the information disclosed and, in certain instances, seek further and better particulars. Of course, the purchaser should always seek to avoid the situation in which the disclosure letter is delivered at the eleventh hour and should press the seller to deliver an early draft so that the due diligence process can get under way in a meaningful fashion.

Certificates of title

One area of due diligence which legal advisers often undertake is to investigate title to the target company's properties. As an alternative to this, it may be possible, where the target company's existing solicitors are familiar with the title to its properties, to arrange for those solicitors to deliver certificates of title

effectively confirming the legal ownership of such properties. One advantage
of certificates of title is that they can
sometimes be quicker and cheaper than
an investigation because the information is already known by the solicitors
concerned. Another advantage is the
professional indemnity insurance cover
of the solicitors giving the certificate.

> **One advantage of certificates of title is that they can sometimes be quicker and cheaper than an investigation because the information is already known by the solicitors concerned.**

Commissioning specialist reports

Depending on the nature of the target company's business it may be necessary for the purchaser to instruct specialist advisers to produce reports on particular aspects of the business (e.g. environmental risk-assessment reports). These reports invariably require the longest lead time in any part of the transaction, so the purchaser should normally commission these reports as soon as possible (particularly where such reports cannot be produced without personal visits by the specialist advisers to the target company's premises).

Public information

There is a great deal of information which can be obtained about a target company from public sources. The one advantage of such information is that the purchaser is not reliant on the co-operation of the seller. Moreover, independent checks can be run to verify the information which the seller provides himself.

The extent of legal due diligence

It is possible to purchase a company relying only on warranties and indemnities. In such circumstances the information disclosed by the seller to qualify the warranties will be the only material available to the purchaser upon which his decision will be based. However, most purchasers prefer to know about problems beforehand and not to have to sue the seller after completion for concealing material facts.

Balanced against the 'warranties only' approach is the question of the costs of the independent verification of facts. In many instances, the commercial imperative is to concentrate on the areas perceived to be the most important to the business being acquired. Due diligence reports do not have to relate to all

> **The professional adviser always faces the risk of allegations of professional negligence if things go wrong in relation to a matter which could have been researched independently beforehand.**

aspects of the target's affairs. Special areas of concern can be identified for discreet investigation.

The nature of the due diligence programme may also depend on the type of purchaser. For example, a purchaser in the same or similar field of business as the target company may feel more relaxed about the level and scope of due diligence required than, say, a venture capital led acquisition team.

Because many independent checks can be run, the professional adviser always faces the risk of allegations of professional negligence if things go wrong in relation to a matter which could have been researched independently beforehand. This may be brought sharply into focus if the purchaser's claims under the warranties cannot be pursued for any reason (the seller may be insolvent, for example). The test at law is what a reasonable professional would have done in the circumstances. In practice, it makes sense for professionals to agree the extent of any due diligence in advance with the purchaser, not only to agree that the costs can be incurred but also to confirm what is expected of the professional and who will be responsible for regulating the information flow. Leaving the precise extent of any due diligence programme unidentified can be fraught with problems. As a consequence of this, it is becoming increasingly common for purchasers and their advisers to enter into formal letters of engagement stipulating exactly what work will be carried out in relation to a due diligence investigation. It is likely that this trend will continue.

Leaving aside the question of the costs of due diligence, one would have thought that the more extensive the due diligence exercise the more likely it is that the purchaser will find protection. However, rather perversely, it may be the case that a purchaser's due diligence may actually undermine warranty claims. The reason for this can lie in the terms of the acquisition agreement. Purchaser-drafted acquisition agreements often provide that the purchaser's prior knowledge of a particular matter is no defence by the seller to warranty claims, unless the matter is actually disclosed in the disclosure letter. This is a common approach, so that only matters disclosed in the formal disclosure letter are treated as qualifying the warranties contained in the sale agreement. The commercial objective is obvious: the parties are clear as to the warranties given in the sale agreement, and to the disclosures which qualify them. However, the courts have not always been entirely comfortable with this approach. For instance in *Eurocopy Plc* v *Teesdale and Others* the court was of the view that a purchaser's knowledge of a particular matter may nevertheless be relevant to the assessment of damages in respect of his warranty claims. The judge in the case offered the opinion that the purchaser's knowledge outside the matters disclosed in the disclosure letter may be pertinent in assessing (i.e. reducing) the purchaser's claim for breach of warranty. If this case is indicative of the approach which will be followed by the courts, it makes the practice of purchasers refusing to accept disclosures made in earlier drafts of a disclosure letter a dangerous procedure. Although not qualifying the warranties formally in terms of the sale agreement, the court may nevertheless take the purchaser's actual prior knowledge into account in assessing the damage he suffered. The answer in practice is for the purchaser to allow the relevant information to be included in the disclosure letter so that it can be identified and then to seek separate indemnities in the sale agreement against any liabilities flowing from the circumstances in question.

> **The answer in practice is for the purchaser to allow the relevant information to be included in the disclosure letter so that it can be identified and then to seek separate indemnities in the sale agreement against any liabilities flowing from the circumstances in question.**

Information gathering 22

Time constraints

number of time constraints are likely to affect the due diligence process.

Competitive offers

The purchaser's desire to secure the deal ahead of a competing bidder may mean that there is only minimal time to conduct due diligence investigations.

Lock-out periods

Many potential purchasers will attempt to negotiate a lock-out period, that is a period during which the seller agrees not to discuss the sale with other interested parties or encourage such interest. The sanction for breaking the undertaking is often that the seller will pay the potential purchaser's due diligence costs and also possibly pay a 'break fee'. A lock-out period will give the purchaser a priority period during which it can conduct due diligence and, if appropriate, conclude the purchase.

Confidentiality agreements

Some sellers will not release any information until a confidentiality agreement has been signed by the purchaser. Although there are often additional provisions, the seller will want such an agreement to require the purchaser and his advisers to keep all disclosed information confidential, to use the information only for assessing the prospective transaction and for the return of all documents (including copies) at the seller's request or if the purchaser decides not to proceed.

These agreements can take time to negotiate, during which the due diligence exercise can be held up. There is perhaps an unfortunate trend for these agreements to become excessively complicated and onerous, which often frustrates a quick start to the transaction.

What are the obstacles to LDD?

Sensitive information

The seller's desire to hold back on sensitive commercial information (for example, detailed customer information) is perhaps understandable, but unfortunately it may lead to last minute negotiations if the information disclosed is adverse to the interests of the purchaser or, even worse for all concerned, an abortive deal.

Competing buyers

Where there are competing buyers it is likely the seller will control the information flow to make sure that each potential buyer is given an equal opportunity to make a bid, and consummate the transaction. In these circumstances, a purchaser can only go as fast as the seller permits.

Restricting access to the seller's employees

The seller may wish to keep the proposed sale confidential from employees. If this extends to top management then it makes any meaningful due diligence virtually impossible. It will certainly prevent any personal visits to the target's premises. Only once top executives are informed will the purchaser be able to obtain information which the seller cannot itself extract without raising suspicions.

Third-party consents

At an early stage the purchaser should ask the seller whether the target company is itself bound by any confidentiality obligations to third parties. These might arise, for example, as a consequence of joint venture or other business partnership agreements and may prevent the target company disclosing critical business information to the prospective purchaser without the other contracting party's consent. Early identification of any such problem is essential. Similarly, certain information may be protected by data protection legislation and this will need to be identified.

Available information sources

These can be separated into three categories:

1 publicly available information;
2 direct investigations (see Chapter 21);
3 data rooms (see Chapter 21).

Publicly available information

This information falls under a number of headings. While most of the sources of information described below are those relevant to the UK, equivalent sources are likely to be available in other jurisdictions.

Property

- *Registered or unregistered?* If the property is registered, a search of the Land Registry will reveal the owner, the benefits attaching to the land and any encumbrances such as mortgages and restrictive covenants. It will also reveal a conclusive file plan showing the boundaries of the property. If the property is unregistered, a public index search at the Land Registry will reveal that it is unregistered. Investigation of title of unregistered land can only be accomplished by an inspection of the title deeds. A search of the Land Registry will reveal whether there are any cautions against first registration of the unregistered land.

  A search should be made at the Land Charges Department if the land is unregistered. The search is made against the name of the owner of the property, not the property itself. The search will reveal details of mortgages, restrictive covenants, adverse easements, matrimonial land charges, etc. In the case of a corporate owner of unregistered land, a search should be made at the Companies Registry to see if there are any registered charges.

- *Local Authority Searches (including Local Land Charges Registry).* These show the usual matters (such as road building projects, advance warning of compulsory purchase orders, etc.) which may affect the property. The local land charges registry will reveal matters such as planning enforcement notices and whether the building is listed or in a conservation area. These searches should be made irrespective of whether the property is registered or unregistered.

- *Less Usual Property Searches.* Various specialist searches may be undertaken in relation to areas of the country where there are coal mines, salt mines or other excavations, common land, rivers and canals with possible responsibility for river banks and canal walls, and proximity to railways and sources of industrial discharges.

In relation to property, the general point should be remembered that legally the compensation protections given by official searches to a purchaser of land are not available to the purchaser of shares in a company owning the property.

163

Warranties and indemnities are still therefore necessary to provide the purchaser with appropriate legal protection from the seller.

Companies registration office

This will reveal details of the target company's constitution, shareholders, officers, etc. It will also give details of any charges registered against the target company. However, because of the 21-day registration period, charges executed but not yet registered within the 21 days will not be revealed. A search will also reveal the latest filed audited accounts and any notices of appointments of receivers and liquidators. The registrar is now in the practice of issuing certificates of good standing and certified copies of such things as the registered memorandum and articles of association which sometimes provides useful comfort to overseas buyers.

Bankruptcy search at land charges registry

If the purchaser wants to check whether any individual sellers or directors have any bankruptcy proceedings outstanding or pending, a search can be made against their names at the Land Charges Registry.

Judgments/winding-up petitions entered

Searches can be made at court to establish whether the target company has had any winding-up petitions entered against it. Claim forms (writs) and particulars of claim in relation to outstanding litigation are open documents (copies can be obtained from the court file) provided that they have been served, and judgments and orders similarly can be obtained if the judgment or order was given in open court. Such searches may be made in particular where litigation has been disclosed to the purchaser and the purchaser wishes to verify the status of the action.

The potential passing-off of third parties' unregistered trading names is always a possible problem because these cannot be searched against at a central registry.

Special searches and enquiries

In addition to the above, which are probably regarded as the most usual searches, there are special investigations which may be made. Some of these are identified below.

- *Patent Office, Trade Marks Registry, Design Registry.* Searches can be made at these registries not only to verify that the target company owns the intellectual property rights it says it owns, but also to search for potential infringement of third parties' intellectual property rights. The potential passing-off of third parties' unregistered trading names is always a possible problem because these cannot be searched against at a central registry. A practical search of sources such as *Yellow Pages*, trade journals and registers may, however, reveal an obvious problem.

- *Search for similar company names.* Some of the company search agencies offer this service to search for company names similar or phonetically similar to that of the target. This may help to identify possible passing-off problems with registered company names.

- *Credit reference agencies.* These will provide a credit risk assessment of the target company and demonstrate how it is regarded by the wider business community.

- *Register of Disqualified Directors.* This is kept at Companies House and will show if a person has been disqualified from acting as a director. As a practical tip, it helps to have the address and date of birth of the director to get an exact match against the register.

- *Financial Services Authority Register.* This is kept by the Financial Services Authority and will tell the enquirer if a particular organization has permission to carry on regulated activities for the purposes of the Financial Services and Markets Act 2000 (a search can be carried out online at www.fsa.gov.uk).

- *Special licences.* If the target company requires a special licence to carry on business, then it should be verified that this is in force and not subject to pending revocation. At the same time it should be checked whether the acquisition will affect the licence in any way.

- *Special accreditations.* If the target company trades on the fact that it has a special accreditation, for example that it complies with a specific British Standard, this should be checked. In some cases the continuity of the target company's contracts may depend upon the standard remaining in force.

As a practical tip, it helps to have the address and date of birth of the director to get an exact match against the register.

- *Membership of trade organizations.* Similarly, if the target company trades on the back of membership of a specific trade organization, particularly a prestigious one, it should be checked whether it is in good standing with that organization.

- *Adherence to codes of practice.* If the target company professes to adhere to a particular code of practice, check with the relevant body, if you can, that there have been no complaints about any failure to comply with that code of practice by the target company.

- *Qualifications of key individuals.* It might be worth checking that key individuals are as qualified as they say they are. Universities and professional organizations will often confirm whether or not a particular individual holds a specified qualification.

- *Others (e.g. Ships Registry).* The Ships Registry is not conclusive of ownership but it will show encumbrances such as charges and hire purchase agreements against vessels.

- *The Internet.* Searching the target company's website can be a useful source of information as can searching against its name generally on the Internet.

There have been numerous cases of individuals registering Internet domain names or addresses which include or which are confusingly similar to names of well-known corporations.

The Internet has become the international system of choice for exchanging electronic mail. Internet addresses have become as important as postal addresses. There have been numerous cases of individuals registering Internet domain names or addresses which include or which are confusingly similar to names of well-known corporations. Although this will often amount to passing off or trade-mark infringement of others' trading names, a prudent purchaser will check what steps the target has taken to protect its name from such activity, and will search the Internet to see whether any obvious problems already exist.

Commercial database information

Sometimes, useful information can be thrown up about a target company from a commercial database which incorporates such things as news clippings, analysts' reports and similar material. It is surprising how much information is in the public domain but a powerful search tool is often needed to quickly scan the available information. Some commercial databases are extremely efficient in this respect and their usefulness in due diligence investigations should not be overlooked. Some are available free over the Internet. Others are available by subscription.

Potential problems 23

Overseas or cross-border transactions

The overseas aspects of a transaction should not be forgotten. One of the first questions a purchaser should ask is whether the target company has any subsidiaries or assets situated abroad. If so, the transaction may throw up a number of added challenges to the due diligence programme.

Legal

It may be necessary to conduct local due diligence in the jurisdiction concerned. Overseas lawyers will need to be appointed and it will be necessary for them to identify for the purchaser what equivalent searches and enquiries can be made in the local jurisdiction and what, if any, impact local law will have on the transaction.

Practical

There may be added difficulties relating to language, the added number of people involved and time differences.

Cultural

In some jurisdictions investigations of a level which have now become good practice in the UK or USA, for example, may be seen as damaging the spirit of mutual trust between seller and purchaser or even as a sign of mistrust or bad faith on the part of the purchaser. The purchaser and his advisers should be sensitive to these issues.

> In some jurisdictions investigations of a level which have now become good practice in the UK or USA, for example, may be seen as damaging the spirit of mutual trust between seller and purchaser.

Spotting the danger signs

Every target company will be different and will throw up its own problems. Most legal advisers working in this area will have detailed checklists to assist them with any due diligence programme. An example is contained in the

Appendix. Whilst these are useful, much will depend upon training and experience. Instinct and a healthy scepticism can be useful! The due diligence team should ideally include relevant specialists and people with knowledge of the target company's field of business, but members with general commercial experience can also be helpful.

The shortcomings of due diligence

The business case for prior knowledge about an acquisition target is compelling, but the seller may not tell the purchaser the truth or the whole story in response to questions. The purchaser may be left exposed and need to consider specific legal protection as well.

Why is legal protection necessary?

There are three principal reasons why legal protection is advisable in connection with the purchase of a company.

The caveat emptor or 'buyer beware' principle

In jurisdictions applying the common law legal system, such as that of the UK, the USA, and the British Commonwealth countries, it is usually the case that virtually no terms are implied in favour of a purchaser of shares in a target company. Consequently, protection must be dealt with by investigation and express contractual provision. In countries applying the civil code legal system, such as much of continental Europe, more terms are implied but express contractual protection is often seen as necessary in addition.

> **Purchasers often believe, erroneously, that they can rely on the audited accounts of the target company such that, if those accounts prove to have been negligently audited, a purchaser can sue the auditors for any fall in value of the target company as a result.**

Reliance on target company's accounts

Purchasers often believe, erroneously, that they can rely on the audited accounts of the target company such that, if those accounts prove to have been negligently audited, a purchaser can sue the auditors for any fall in value of the target company as a result. There is a long line of authority beginning with the landmark decision in *Caparo Industries plc* v *Dickman and Others*, (1990) 2 WLR 358, which established the principle that auditors owe their duties to the company and not to any purchaser of, or investor in, its shares. In the absence of an express representation by the auditors to the purchaser upon which it was intended the purchaser should rely, the purchaser is unlikely to recover damages from the auditors in these circumstances.

Case study – Caparo Industries plc v Dickman and Others (1990)

The facts

Fidelity plc (Fidelity), a manufacturer and vendor of electrical equipment, announced disappointing results for 1984 which led to a sharp fall in the price of its shares. Following the announcement, Caparo Industries plc (Caparo) began in June 1984 to purchase Fidelity's shares, culminating in a successful takeover bid in October 1984. Caparo subsequently claimed it had relied on accounts certified by Fidelity's auditors, Touche Ross & Co (Touche Ross), which had overstated Fidelity's profits and were negligently audited. Had it known the true position, Caparo claimed, it would not have made the bid at the price it did, or indeed at all. Caparo also claimed that, as Fidelity's profits were not as high as projected and as its share price had fallen significantly, Touche Ross should have known that Fidelity was susceptible to a takeover bid and thus potential purchasers such as itself would rely on the accuracy of the audited accounts.

The law of negligence

The law of negligence is part of the common law and follows the precedents of previously decided cases. Previous cases showed that a claimant will only succeed in suing a professional person for negligent statements if the claimant can establish a close enough relationship ('proximity') between him and the professional.

The decision

The House of Lords decided unanimously that sufficient proximity did not exist between Touche Ross and Caparo to make Touche Ross liable in negligence, and that the statutory requirement for an audit does not make auditors liable to a company's actual or potential shareholders.

Case study – Caparo Industries plc v Dickman and Others (1990) (continued)

In particular, it was held that auditors of a public company owe no general duty of care to individual shareholders or members of the public who rely on the accounts when dealing in the company's shares. If a duty of care were owed so widely the House of Lords acknowledged that it would unfairly subject auditors to 'liability in an indeterminate amount for an indeterminate time to an indeterminate class'.

No special relationship giving rise to liability to a purchaser follows from the fact that a company is known by the auditors to be vulnerable to takeover.

When liability may arise

The House of Lords accepted that auditors may be liable to investors in negligence only if sufficient proximity is found to exist. This may arise where an auditor 'assumes responsibility' (e.g. acknowledges that a purchaser will rely on the accounts). It may also arise when the auditors know that a purchaser specifically or as a member of an identifiable class is 'very likely' to rely on the accounts in deciding whether to enter into a particular transaction or type of transaction.

Misrepresentation by a seller

Oral misrepresentations are notoriously difficult to prove and so purchasers usually seek express written representations (or 'warranties') in the sale agreement.

Where the purchaser has been induced to enter into the sale agreement by a prior misrepresentation, the purchaser may be able to rescind the sale and/or claim damages. However, oral misrepresentations are notoriously difficult to prove and so purchasers usually seek express written representations (or 'warranties') in the sale agreement.

The legal underpinning of due diligence

Legal protection usually takes two forms: warranties and indemnities.

Warranties

Warranties are statements of fact which the seller confirms to the purchaser as being true, for example, that the target company is not involved in any litigation. If the seller knows that this is not true, the convention is not to amend the warranty but instead to disclose the real facts (e.g. the details of the actual litigation) in a separate letter called the disclosure letter. The effect of the seller making accurate disclosure of matters which form exceptions to the warranties is that the seller will not incur any liability under the warranties.

> Warranties are statements of fact which the seller confirms to the purchaser as being true. If the seller knows that this is not true, the convention is not to amend the warranty but instead to disclose the real facts.

The warranties have two principal functions. The first is mechanical in the sense of the collection of useful information about the target company in the form of the disclosure letter. The second is contractual, that is to provide the purchaser with compensation for undisclosed liabilities. To the extent that the seller does not disclose facts which are necessary to qualify the warranties properly then, subject to proving his loss, the purchaser will be entitled to damages to put himself back in the position he would have been had the warranty been true.

A subsidiary consequence of warranties and the disclosure process is price adjustment. If liabilities which were previously unknown to the purchaser are disclosed, then he may want compensation for this in the form of an adjustment of the purchase price before the acquisition is completed.

Indemnities

An indemnity is an obligation to hold the purchaser harmless from a particular liability. An indemnity provides compensation even if the liability in question is disclosed to the purchaser in the disclosure letter. The sale agreement can identify the particular problem and provide that, if that liability crystallizes, the purchaser will be compensated for the loss the purchaser suffers. Indemnities enable the purchaser to adopt a 'wait and see' policy and can sometimes be a useful compromise instead of a price adjustment, particularly where the liability in question is contingent and it is uncertain to what extent, if at all, the liability will crystallize.

A straightforward indemnity in favour of the purchaser is not always the answer for the simple reason that the entity directly suffering the loss is likely to be the target company. The purchaser suffers only indirect loss as a result of

The sale agreement can identify the particular problem and provide that, if that liability crystallizes, the purchaser will be compensated for the loss the purchaser suffers.

the fall in value of the shares he has acquired. This sometimes leads a purchaser to request the seller to indemnify the target company directly. The problem with this is that any payment under the indemnity would be a taxable receipt in the hands of the target company such that it would be necessary to gross up the payment in order to arrange for an amount equal to the loss to be received by the target company net of tax. In practice, this problem is often circumvented by the seller entering into a payment covenant with the purchaser agreeing to pay the purchaser a sum equal to the loss falling on the target company. Any resulting payment is usually treated as an adjustment of the purchase price as between the seller and the purchaser rather than a taxable receipt by the target company.

Both warranties and indemnities can be backed up by a retention from the purchase price for a stipulated period after completion of the sale, against which the purchaser can call in respect of *bona fide* warranty and indemnity claims.

Special legal due diligence **24** obligations

Legal obligations of recipients of due diligence information

number of obligations can arise.

Duty of confidentiality

In most cases a duty of confidentiality is probably implied by English law in any event, but it is quite often dealt with in a formal confidentiality agreement. A purchaser who misuses confidential information may face an action for damages or an injunction to restrain his unlawful use of that information.

Specific contractual covenants

These may include covenants given by the purchaser not to solicit any of the target company's customers or employees and may be contained as separate undertakings in a confidentiality agreement. They usually bite not only during the due diligence period but also for a stated period after an abortive transaction.

Competitive research and development

Where the purchaser and the target company are competitors in an industry which requires ongoing and secret research and development, an abortive transaction may lead to allegations from the seller that the purchaser has used the potential transaction as a ruse to gain access to the target company's ideas. Specific agreements can be developed to cover this possibility and to establish an agreed dispute resolution procedure in the event of such an allegation.

> **Where the purchaser and the target company are competitors in an industry which requires ongoing and secret research and development, an abortive transaction may lead to allegations from the seller.**

175

Insider dealing

If either the purchaser's or the seller's securities are traded on the London Stock Exchange or other securities market, then the proposed transaction may be price-sensitive in relation to those securities. An insider should not therefore deal or pass information to a third party who is likely to deal in the securities until the transaction is made public and ceases to be price-sensitive.

Public bids: a special case

Where a UK company is listed or is a widely held public company, the City Code on Takeovers and Mergers will govern the takeover. Due diligence programmes in relation to public companies have their own special features. In theory, the increased disclosure requirements imposed by the Listing Rules of the UK Listing Authority should ensure that all information which affects the price of the securities in the target company is in the public domain. If that is true then due diligence should be a matter of trawling through published documents and announcements. In practice, life can be very different – and Maxwell Communications is an obvious example of where the theory can break down.

A potential bidder for a public company should remember the decision in *Caparo* v. *Dickman and Others* (Chapter 23). Generally speaking, the target's accounts may not be relied upon by the bidder to provide a claim against the auditors of the target company in the event that the accounts prove to have been negligently audited.

Where the bid is recommended by the target's board of directors, it will usually be possible to undertake a due diligence exercise, although the bidder will normally be requested to sign appropriate confidentiality undertakings. In the case of a hostile bid, however, the minimum of co-operation can be expected from the target's board and the bidder must in these circumstances rely essentially on publicly available information about the target company.

Even if the offer is recommended by the target's board, warranties and indemnities are unlikely to be given unless there is a controlling shareholder who is prepared to give them. The directors of a target company are unlikely to be willing to incur legal liability in relation to warranties and indemnities, especially if they have no significant shareholdings and will not benefit financially to any material extent from the offer.

A competitive offeror's right to information under Rule 20 of the City Code can give rise to problems in relation to due diligence programmes in connection with public bids. Rule 20 provides that where there are competitive bids one of which is recommended and the other is hostile, the target company is required to supply the same information to the hostile bidder as that supplied to the recommended bidder. However, this right is limited by the requirement that the hostile bidder cannot ask in general terms

A competitive offeror's right to information under Rule 20 of the City Code can give rise to problems in relation to due diligence programmes in connection with public bids.

for all information supplied to the recommended bidder but can only ask specific questions to which it needs answers.

This rule, of course, may act as a constraint on a due diligence exercise. The target company may be reluctant to disclose sensitive information to a preferred bidder in case it gets into the hands of another bidder which is an industry competitor.

Case study – HSBC's offer for Midland Bank plc

In April 1992 the Hong Kong & Shanghai Bank announced a recommended offer for Midland Bank plc. In response to this, Lloyds Bank plc announced that it was considering making an offer for Midland.

Mindful no doubt of the scope of Rule 20 of the City Code, Lloyds made it a precondition of it making an offer for Midland that Lloyds should receive all the information which HSBC had received from Midland during the course of their discussions leading up to the offer. Following a request from Lloyds for this information, the board of Midland became very concerned that Lloyds, as a result, could come into possession of some very sensitive commercial information. There was no dispute that Lloyds was a *'bona fide* potential offeror' for the purposes of the Rule.

Midland asked the Panel to waive or modify the requirement The Executive of the Panel refused. The Panel, on appeal by Midland from the decision of the Executive, decided not to modify the Rule. Midland was required by the Panel to hand over to Lloyds the information which had previously been passed to HSBC.

The Panel, whose main responsibility is to protect the interests of shareholders in connection with takeover bids, took the view that the likelihood of damage being done to Midland shareholders was greater if the relevant information was to be withheld than if it were to be given to Lloyds. The Panel pointed out that Midland should have been aware of the Rule and that as a result other less welcome potential offerors could become entitled to request the information which it had passed to HSBC. Midland should have borne this in mind when deciding to pass sensitive information to HSBC.

Post-acquisition due diligence

This is a part of the due diligence programme which is often overlooked. The main weakness it suffers from is communication problems. Very often the acquisition team moves on to the next deal and is not the same group of people that is given responsibility for managing the business of the target company after completion. It is essential that somebody is given responsibility in such circumstances for identifying possible warranty and indemnity claims which may come to light after completion. The usual reaction of a manager to a business problem is to solve it rather than to consider whether it was a problem which was extant at completion and which could be the subject of a legal claim.

In connection with warranty and indemnity claims, the purchaser's team should watch any applicable time limits. The statutory limitation period for notifying warranty and indemnity claims is six years from the sale in the case of a document executed under hand and 12 years for a deed. These periods can be shortened by contract, and commonly the limitation periods negotiated in sale agreements can be as low as two years in relation to commercial warranties but often up to six years for taxation warranties and indemnities (for the simple reason that the Inland Revenue has six years in which to come back to the target). Diarising these limitation periods therefore becomes a vital part of the post-acquisition due diligence procedure.

It is not uncommon for the sale agreement to contain formal notification procedures for dealing with warranty and indemnity claims. There might also be provisions for resolving any claims by reference to an expert or by arbitration. The purchaser should ensure that it complies with all relevant procedures in accordance with the sale agreement.

The Seller's View 25

Legal issues

There are various issues to be considered by a seller facing a due diligence investigation.

Antecedent investigations

There are many sources of information for a potential purchaser of a company. Moreover, skilful private investigators may be able to uncover surprisingly sensitive and confidential information about the target company, so the seller should not exaggerate the target company's position. The purchaser may sometimes know more than the seller!

> Skilful private investigators may be able to uncover surprisingly sensitive and confidential information about the target company, so the seller should not exaggerate the target company's position.

Covert operations

Private investigators use all sorts of methods to obtain information. A seller should watch out for any unusual approaches, no matter how innocent and plausible they appear to be, during the negotiating period.

Code names

It is a very useful discipline to insist that all parties to the proposed sale use agreed code names. Very often code names can help protect the identity of the parties and the target company, should any sensitive correspondence or other written material fall into the wrong hands.

Channels of communication

Where confidentiality from employees is important to the seller, the seller should insist on strict channels of communication. Normally these would be via the seller or only with top-level management of the target company.

Check existing restrictions on disclosure

The seller should check to make sure that any information it passes to the potential buyer concerning the target company is not disseminated in breach of any non-disclosure obligations to third parties.

As mentioned earlier, it may be that the target company is bound by obligations of confidentiality to third parties pursuant to joint venture or business partnership agreements. The seller should check the situation to make sure that any information it passes to the potential buyer concerning the target company is not disseminated in breach of any non-disclosure obligations to third parties.

Confidentiality agreement

It is always a wise precaution for the seller to insist that the purchaser signs a confidentiality agreement at the outset. Under the terms of such an agreement the seller will make it clear that the information concerning the target company which is given to the purchaser or its advisers is only imparted for the purpose of enabling the purchaser to make an offer for the target company and conduct the purchase negotiations. Moreover, the seller will also wish to ensure that the purchaser does not disclose the fact that the target company is up for sale, if the seller wishes to avoid that fact becoming public knowledge.

Restrictions on approaches to other parties

Much damage can be done if the purchaser approaches existing and former customers, suppliers, competitors and employees as an adjunct to its investigations into the target company. In return for disclosing confidential information to the potential purchaser, the seller might require the potential purchaser to enter into appropriate restrictions as part of the confidentiality agreement.

Data rooms

Where there are competing potential buyers, the seller might use a data room to make information available to enable the potential buyers to put in indicative bids. Usually this information may not be taken out of the data room, and this helps to prevent unnecessary dissemination of confidential information to those bidders who prove in the event to be unsuccessful.

Keep your legal adviser informed

From the seller's perspective, the commercial imperative is proper disclosure. It is therefore very important that all information which is supplied to the purchaser or its advisers is also supplied to the seller's solicitor so that he can include it in the formal disclosure letter. In this respect, personal visits can often be dangerous because the potential buyer has access to information which may not necessarily be copied to the seller's solicitor. Discipline and co-ordination are required in this area.

> From the seller's perspective, the commercial imperative is proper disclosure. It is therefore very important that all information which is supplied to the purchaser or its advisers is also supplied to the seller's solicitor so that he can include it in the formal disclosure letter.

Price re-negotiations

Remember that disclosure may lead to a price adjustment.

Disclosure discipline

It is tempting for the seller to throw as much information as possible into the disclosure letter. However, the seller should be disciplined in this respect as the contents of the disclosure letter will themselves often be warranted as part of the sale and purchase agreement. Statements which cannot be verified properly should be used with caution.

Beware purchaser-introduced disclosure documents

The purchaser may itself offer to include certain information in the disclosure letter, and may do so on the basis of a statement that the purchaser is relying on certain information and that it would be helpful for the seller as part of his disclosure obligation. The problem is that some documents may not be appropriate for a disclosure letter. For example, any sale memorandum which has been prepared on the company may not have been properly verified and may contain a certain amount of advertising puff or speculation. Moreover, any accountants' report, which is often extremely detailed, can only safely be incorporated if it is verified by the target's top management. But even then some of the material (particularly opinions) in the report may not be appropriate to be warranted as accurate as part of the disclosure letter.

> Statements which cannot be verified properly should be used with caution.

181

Environmental due diligence **26**

Why conduct environmental due diligence?

This section sits within the legal due diligence part of this book as many of the issues it raises have a bearing on any legal due diligence process. It considers the topic of environmental due diligence from the point of view of a *purchaser*.

The theory that the more extensive the contractual protection provided the less need there is to carry out due diligence is not a good rule of thumb in the area of environmental due diligence. First, there is the usual issue that warranties and indemnities are always subject to the seller's standing and the purchaser's ability to enforce them. Secondly, leaving aside the question of contaminated land liabilities which are a common concern, there is the question of whether a business complies with environmental laws. Even if a purchaser gets generous contractual comfort, it will want to know that a regulator is not about to walk in and shut the business down and that the purchaser can continue to operate it lawfully.

It is self-evident that the better the purchaser's knowledge, the better its position for negotiating and for making an evaluation of the business. Further, for some type of liabilities (typically regarding non-contaminated land), sellers are more likely to give indemnities for identified issues rather than broad wholesale indemnities, although this will, of course, depend on the terms of the particular deal.

> There is the usual issue that warranties and indemnities are always subject to the seller's standing and the purchaser's ability to enforce them. There is the question of whether a business complies with environmental laws. Even if a purchaser gets generous contractual comfort, it will want to know that a regulator is not about to walk in and shut the business down and that the purchaser can continue to operate it lawfully.

Relationships between advisers

The relationship between an environmental lawyer and an environmental consultant can be regarded as similar to that between a solicitor and a surveyor in a residential property transaction. However, this is an oversimplification of the position.

> **An environmental consultant can inspect technical information and equipment and say whether or not it is operated in compliance with the applicable permit, i.e. whether there is a breach of law. However, the lawyer will advise on the legal consequences of this breach and draft and negotiate any contractual protection required.**

Environmental consultants are usually retained to inspect current sites and current operations and to identify whether there is any pollution associated with those sites and operations, whether the operations comply with permits and regulations and whether there are any impending regulatory changes which will have an impact on operations. Their role is legal to an extent. For example, an environmental consultant can inspect technical information and equipment and say whether or not it is operated in compliance with the applicable permit, i.e. whether there is a breach of law. However, the lawyer will advise on the legal consequences of this breach and draft and negotiate any contractual protection required. That said, it is important to note that environmental consultants are not lawyers. For example, their focus will naturally be towards the regulatory regime rather than third-party claims arising under common law. Hence, it will usually be the lawyer (on the basis of the information provided in disclosure or by the environmental consultant) who will push forward enquiries in this regard including asking the consultant for his technical input. We have recently noted environmental consultants stepping into the area of contaminated land law and using their analysis of the legal position to conclude that there is no risk or to justify not conducting due diligence in respect of a piece of land. In each case the legal analysis was wrong. In short, it is the consultant's job to assess whether or not any contamination is or is likely to be present and the lawyer's job to advise on the legal consequences including the consequences of not doing any due diligence.

Environmental consultants' fees tend to be cheaper (often significantly) than those of commercial lawyers and it is usually money well spent to get a Phase 1 audit (i.e. non-intrusive audit in respect of current operations and sites). The alternative is often a lawyer spending a lot of time trying to elicit information through disclosure and/or drafting and/or negotiating in a factual vacuum. Also, sellers are not well disposed to purchasers who conduct technical due diligence and ask for a significant indemnity – this can be seen as lazy.

Extent of due diligence

The extent of environmental due diligence required will be largely dictated by the nature of the target's operations, the types of properties involved and the stringency of the applicable legal regime. The quality of information provided by the seller may also influence the purchaser's approach. Where environmental issues may affect the target the purchaser should use a specialist lawyer and consider engaging a specialist environmental consultant. A specialist environmental lawyer can advise on the pros and cons of instructing environmental consultants and help them adopt a commercial approach. If in-depth due diligence, for example involving intrusive investigations, is required, the team could include further specialist advisers, such as hydrogeologists. Such specialists usually form part of an environmental consultant's organization and may be accessed through a single representative of the environmental consultants.

The structure of the transaction is a key factor in shaping the due diligence. More particularly, if the transaction is for the purchase of shares rather than assets, the purchaser must remember that it is buying the consequences of a company's history. For some types of environmental liability, notably contaminated land, companies can be retrospectively liable for things they did lawfully and many years ago and in respect of properties they no longer own or occupy. In asset transactions, a purchaser may directly or indirectly acquire some of the seller's environmental liabilities but (subject to any contractual arrangements) in general terms these will only relate to the business being acquired.

> **For some types of environmental liability, notably contaminated land, companies can be retrospectively liable for things they did lawfully and many years ago and in respect of properties they no longer own or occupy.**

It may be difficult to undertake due diligence on a company's history and the seller may not even have the relevant information. In such circumstances a purchaser may want an indemnity to cover liabilities arising from former properties and/or operations.

Lead time

As environmental due diligence often requires visits to sites and examination of publicly available information, long lead times may be necessary. It is usually preferable for the environmental consultant's report to be available prior to legal due diligence taking place, because this will highlight the principal areas of

> **As environmental due diligence often requires visits to sites and examination of publicly available information, long lead times may be necessary.**

concern relating to current operations and sites for which legal protection may be required. It is thus advisable for the purchaser to commission this report as soon as possible. That said, environmental consultants are used to turning Phase 1 audits around quickly to meet transaction deadlines. However, Phase 2 audits will inevitably take longer as they involve mobilizing equipment, digging boreholes, taking samples and also on laboratory turn around times.

In some cases the seller will do Phase 1 audits and provide them to the purchaser or bidders for the target.

Choice of environmental consultants

Care should be taken in engaging environmental consultants. The nature of the due diligence programme will dictate what technical competence and resources are required of the consultant. Environmental lawyers are often in a position to assist in the engagement of suitable environmental consultants and the terms of their appointment.

Terms of engagement

It is important and good practice to appoint the consultant by means of a written appointment and before the work (especially intrusive investigations) starts. It is necessary to set out the scope of the consultant's work – he/she will usually produce a proposal. The terms of engagement should also deal with liability. Generally, environmental consultants' standard terms of engagement are to be avoided because they are usually drafted to minimize the consultant's exposure to the financial consequences of negligence. Points covered usually include insurance, duties of care, extent of the consultants' liability, access to sites and confidentiality. The appointment should require them to maintain appropriate insurance for a specified period of time (typically somewhere between six and 12 years). It is also market practice for consultants to place a total financial cap on their liability. This

> **Generally, environmental consultants' standard terms of engagement are to be avoided because they are usually drafted to minimize the consultant's exposure to the financial consequences of negligence.**

should be negotiated on a case-by-case basis. Increased caps and insurance may result in increased fees, but may be necessary especially if the transaction is being funded externally.

The environmental consultant's report

Environmental consultants will frequently limit liability for reliance upon their report to the purchaser alone. If other parties are intending to rely upon the report, such as funders, this should be expressly negotiated with the consultants. Most consultants are happy to address their report to other parties or to provide deeds of collateral warranty in respect of the work done, provided their total financial cap on liability and other limitations on liability shall apply.

Liability under some environmental laws can arise from a party knowingly permitting pollution. Therefore, the knowledge acquired by a purchaser during due diligence (including that derived from an environmental report) which identifies ongoing pollution could constitute the knowledge element of liability if that purchaser fails to correct that ongoing pollution. Such a report is unlikely to be protected by legal professional privilege and, if relevant, would have to be disclosed in proceedings and thus could be used against the purchaser.

The legal framework for EDD

Environmental consultants by the nature of their role tend to focus on the increasingly stringent legislative framework for environmental protection within which companies operate. However, it is very important to remember that there are also common law liabilities in relation to the environment which must be considered. These liabilities can arise in tort (e.g. for damage caused to neighbours) or in contract (e.g. as a tenant under a lease).

The key areas which are looked at are set out below.

Discharges to the environment

Where a business operates a process that discharges to the environment, the purchaser will wish to be satisfied that the discharges are fully authorized. The regime that applies will be dependent upon the process and often upon the scale of operations. Under the Integrated Pollution Control provisions (Part I of the Environmental Protection Act 1990) discharges to air and water from certain industrial processes are controlled by the Environment Agency and discharges to air from certain other processes are subject to control by the local authority.

Discharges to air and water from certain industrial processes are controlled by the Environment Agency and discharges to air from certain other processes are subject to control by the local authority.

This regime is gradually being replaced by the PPC (Pollution Prevention and Control) regime which is more comprehensive. For the larger more polluting processes it will additionally regulate matters such as waste, noise and odour. Again, the local authority will regulate air emissions from less polluting processes. The number of processes caught by the new regime is wider.

Contaminated land

A company's past operations may have led to contamination of land. This could include sites it currently occupies, sites it occupied in the past and land contaminated by migration of substances from those sites. Under Part II A of the Environmental Protection Act 1990 liability is strict and retrospective – in very general terms (and subject to proof), a company which polluted a site 100 years ago and operated in compliance with the then applicable law and best practice could still be liable to pay for remediation.

Further, a company may incur liabilities in respect of land which it currently occupies even if it did not put the polluting substances there in the first place. This could be as site owner where the polluter cannot be found or if it is deemed to have 'knowingly permitted' the pollution.

Statutory guidance issued under Part II A of the Environmental Protection Act 1990 indicates how liability should be apportioned if there is more than one person who may be liable for contamination caused by a particular pollutant. In particular, the statutory guidance provides for people who 'caused' or 'knowingly permitted' contamination to be able to transfer liability on selling the land in certain situations. For example, by either:

- reducing the purchase price with an express provision stating that the reduction is for remediation of contamination; or
- by providing the purchaser of the land with information about the presence of significant pollutants on that land before sale (in some cases in transactions since the beginning of 1990, a purchaser who is permitted to carry out its own investigations will be deemed to have acquired knowledge about the presence of substances on the land).

These provisions are relevant on an asset purchase. The crucial point to note is that if the contract is silent, the law may still operate to transfer the seller's liabilities for contaminated land to the purchaser. However, the statutory guidance only relates to Part II A of the Environmental Protection Act 1990, and liabilities for contaminated land can arise under other legislation or the common law. For example, a purchaser who buys land causing ongoing pollution may become liable in its own right as a 'knowing polluter' or for adopting or continuing a nuisance. Moreover, contaminated land which is causing ongoing water pollution could result in criminal liability. Therefore, although it is important to understand the implications of acquiring information for the purposes of Part II A of the Environmental Protection Act 1990, usually the best practice will be to conduct appropriate due diligence and make express provision in the contract for the allocation and apportionment of contaminated risk.

Discharges to water may require consent from the Environment Agency under the Water Resources Act 1991. Discharges to sewer are likely to require a consent under the Water Industry Act 1991 from the relevant water undertaker.

Waste

The purchaser will wish to be satisfied that waste disposal from the operations is conducted in accordance with the law as well as assessing the costs of such disposal. The management of waste on a site, as well as disposal, could be subject to licensing requirements under Part II of the Environmental Protection Act 1990.

It is also important to establish whether the target is caught by the Producer Responsibility Obligations (Packaging Waste) Regulations 1997 and that it is complying and to assess the costs of compliance.

Other

In addition to the above, there are several other aspects of business operation that may require environmental permits, or could represent a cost to the business including, among others, the right to abstract water and the use of radioactive materials. There are also health and safety and planning aspects to consider relating to, for example, the storage of hazardous materials, the identification and management of asbestos and labelling of hazardous materials.

Compliance with environmental permits is not a defence to damage caused to third parties.

Civil consequences

As stated above, if a business causes damage to third parties, there may be liabilities in tort. Compliance with environmental permits is not a defence to damage caused to third parties. Also the target, if the purchaser is acquiring a company, may have liabilities under contract, for instance, other disposal contracts. Potential liabilities under leases could arise if the purchaser is acquiring a company which is a tenant or if taking an assignment of a lease on an asset transaction.

Criminal and regulatory consequences

Many breaches of environmental legislation and permits can result in criminal liabilities. They can also result in the risk of the business being shut down. Further, sometimes compliance can be expensive or technologically difficult and it is important in due diligence to ask about forthcoming legislation or variations to permits which could impact on costs or operations. For example, there may be a requirement to buy new expensive emission abatement equipment.

There is a risk that the obsession with contaminated land means that people lose sight of these issues and assume that only transactions involving brownfield sites will involve environmental issues.

There is a risk that the obsession with contaminated land means that people lose sight of these issues and assume that only transactions involving brownfield sites will involve environmental issues. Retailers, for example, will be caught by the laws relating to waste and packaging.

Sources of information

The seller's disclosure/data room

Based on a knowledge of the seller's operations, it should be possible to identify the categories of information that would ideally be required to carry out the due diligence programme. Careful evaluation of material and comparison with what might be expected to be available often leads to the discovery of missing items. Also, as discussed above, sellers often cannot produce a lot of information on potential liabilities arising from historic operations.

Internal reports and audits (as well as those carried out by external consultants) can be useful in identifying areas that have concerned the seller. Also, correspondence with regulatory authorities can indicate the nature of the relationship with that authority and

Sellers often cannot produce a lot of information on potential liabilities arising from historic operations.

the likely policy of the authority in the future. Even though a purchaser can, to some extent, offer a clean slate to the regulatory authorities, previous difficulties can be problematic. The tenor of communications with regulatory authorities is thus an important aspect.

When evaluating environmental reports that are disclosed, it is necessary to consider the reporting party. The quality of environmental consultants involved in reporting can help in determining the value of any report. In addition, it is common in large corporations for central resources to be available to help smaller sites comply with environmental controls. This assistance can be in the form of research or can be given by way of internal consultancy. A purchaser of part only of the business should therefore be aware of the potential costs of continuing research and other environmental activities in the absence of the central corporate facility.

In addition to information provided by the seller, there are several other sources of information about the environmental performance of companies.

Site visits

Where environmental liabilities are likely to be an important aspect of a transaction, a site visit by an environmental consultant and/or someone with relevant technical expertise in the purchaser's organization is essential. The degree to which the site can be inspected will depend upon the nature of the transaction and the time available.

Often at the offer stage it is not possible to carry out a comprehensive sampling exercise (if one is required), but much can be learned by visual examination of the site, observation of the operations carried out there and by speaking to relevant personnel. At the preferred bidder stage, it may be possible to carry out a more comprehensive survey. Also, a site visit without intrusive

Much can be learned by visual examination of the site, observation of the operations carried out there and by speaking to relevant personnel. It's not all about contaminated land.

investigations by an environmental consultant should provide a picture of whether the site operations are in compliance with current legal requirements – it's not all about contaminated land.

Regulatory authorities

Where the target company's operations are subject to control, regulatory authorities such as the Environment Agency, the local authority and water undertakers can be approached for information in the public domain. Information in the public domain should include authorizations, permits and licences, as well as details of enforcement action taken. Also, under Part II A of the Environmental Protection Act 1990, enforcing authorities are required to maintain registers on contaminated land and on service of any remediation notices. Similarly, under the Water Resources Act 1991, registers are required to be held in relation to discharge consents.

> **Where the target company's operations are subject to control, regulatory authorities such as the Environment Agency, the local authority and water undertakers can be approached.**

If particular issues are of concern, it is possible to have a meeting with the regulatory authority. However, it is important not to breach any confidentiality agreement with the seller.

In relation to environmental discharges, in addition to the need for relevant permits, appropriate rights over adjoining property may be necessary to transport effluents to their final point of disposal.

Insurance

It is necessary to determine the extent of insurance cover in assessing environmental risks, as sellers may qualify warranties and indemnities (unlikely) to exclude items that would be covered by insurance. This is usually linked with a requirement that suitable insurance be maintained by the purchaser. That said, at present it is not usual to have insurance for pollution risks and often insurance contains a pollution exclusion.

Where the purchase is by way of shares, the purchaser should retain the benefit of historic insurance cover. Therefore, a purchaser may want to investigate the insurance position. However, doing a full insurance archaeology exercise in the context of a transaction is highly likely to be impracticable and prohibitively expensive unless the seller has already done the work and can provide the information. Further, whether or not cover would be available would depend on the facts of the case, for example whether or not an insurer could avoid liability on the basis of non-disclosure would be determined on a case-by-case basis. Where the purchase is of assets only, there is unlikely to be continuity of historic insurance.

It is necessary to determine the extent of insurance cover in assessing environmental risks, as sellers may qualify warranties and indemnities (unlikely) to exclude items that would be covered by insurance.

Nevertheless, it is now possible to get insurance cover for contaminated land risks and environmental indemnities. Although expensive, this can be useful in unblocking deadlocks in deals.

Evaluation of the due diligence programme

Although the reports from the legal adviser and the environmental consultant should permit the purchaser to evaluate the environmental risks associated with current activities, the position in relation to the past may not be so clear. In doing so, it will be necessary not only to consider the cost of dealing with identified problems, but also the problems associated with future compliance. Regulatory authorities are generally seeking ever greater environmental performance.

Specialist legal advice may be required where parts of the business are in a foreign jurisdiction. In this regard, it should be noted that Scotland, Northern Ireland – and to some extent Wales – are different jurisdictions from England.

Mechanisms for apportioning liability

Once the risks have been evaluated, there are several mechanisms by which liability can be apportioned between the seller and the purchaser. Some examples are:

- a reduction in the purchase price to reflect environmental costs;
- exclusion of certain affected assets or liabilities;
- the provision of environmental warranties;

- the provision of indemnities for specific environmental issues;
- the remediation of environmental problems at the seller's cost prior to or after completion.

NB: the roles can be reversed, with the purchaser required to give indemnities, do remediation, etc. if it gets a good price on the basis that it is taking on pollution risk.

Warranties and Indemnities

Where indemnities are given by the seller in respect of specific works, the seller may require a covenant from the purchaser that the works will be completed within a given time after completion. Carrying out such works at the seller's cost soon after completion is usually to the advantage of the purchaser. The purchaser then knows that the site or the relevant plant and equipment meet prevailing legal requirements.

If the indemnity is for contaminated land liability which may arise in the future, it may be advisable for the purchaser to require a benchmark survey of the contamination at or near to the completion date to form a future reference point. However, the purchaser should not agree that this is deemed to be the full picture as an intrusive survey is a sampling exercise. A consultant could miss a problem without being negligent. Even where this is done, there is always the risk that there may be pollution incidents during the purchaser's tenure, and the passage of time may make the allocation of responsibility for contamination between the seller and the purchaser factually difficult. However, this will depend on the particular circumstances and technical advice can be sought – this may determine whether a benchmark survey is required.

Specialist legal advice may be required where parts of the business are in a foreign jurisdiction. Scotland, Northern Ireland – and to some extent Wales – are different jurisdictions from England.

Warranties provide some contractual protection, but the most important benefit is in eliciting disclosure of information. In assessing the value of warranties, it should be remembered that disclosure against the warranty negates its protection. If material problems are disclosed, the purchaser may request an indemnity or price reduction.

Sufficient time should be allowed for the purchaser to make claims under environmental warranties and indemnities. The time periods in which environmental problems may become apparent are considerable. Time periods for warranties and indemnities in the environmental field vary on a case-by-case basis. In some cases, indemnities may be unlimited in time.

The English market is now fairly familiar with environmental issues in a transaction context and there is some fairly standard drafting, for example defining 'environmental laws', 'permits', 'contamination', etc. However, it is important to note that environmental indemnities (and other contractual provisions) are tailored to the specific transaction and are essentially a bespoke product.

Large liabilities may be involved that make it worthwhile for the seller to contest indemnity claims and potentially therefore, indemnity claims may be expensive and drawn out. As noted above, the passage of time can create evidential difficulties. Environmental claims are often difficult to prove in any event, due to the complexity of the issues involved. Where it is necessary to claim under an environmental indemnity or warranty, considerable evidence of a technical nature may be involved and the matter may be expensive to litigate. Consideration should be given to an expert determination clause for technical matters.

> **Sufficient time should be allowed for the purchaser to make claims under environmental warranties and indemnities. The time periods in which environmental problems may become apparent are considerable.**

Conclusions

Because of the significant potential liabilities involved and the increasingly tough legal regime, environmental due diligence is an increasingly important aspect of the due diligence process. Where environmental risks are likely to arise, it is advisable to carry out a thorough environmental due diligence programme at the earliest opportunity. It will also be necessary to consider carefully as to which party is taking on what risk and for the sale agreement to reflect this.

Seller's perspective

It is clearly in the seller's interest that environmental risks be transferred to the purchaser. It is a matter for commercial evaluation to determine to what extent the liabilities are allocated between the parties.

It is often in the seller's interests to give as full a disclosure as possible in relation to environmental problems. This may, under the contaminated land regime, have the effect of transferring liability to the purchaser. Also, it may speed up the transaction process if the purchaser does not feel that it is struggling to get environmental information. However, good disclosure could lead to the purchaser seeking specific indemnities, but on the other hand patchy disclosure may make a purchaser nervous and ask for broad contractual protection. Further, the more specific the indemnities are, the easier it is to evaluate commercially the impact of such indemnities. In some cases, a seller, especially if there is an auction or bid process, might commission environmental audits itself and arrange for the ultimate purchaser to be able to rely on them.

> **It is often in the seller's interests to give as full a disclosure as possible in relation to environmental problems. This may, under the contaminated land regime, have the effect of transferring liability to the purchaser.**

Pensions due diligence **27**

I f you are buying a company with a pension scheme or whose employees are members of a group pension scheme, it is essential to get specialist legal advice on the scheme and any poten-

tial liabilities. It may also be necessary to obtain expert actuarial advice to quantify the extent of those liabilities. This chapter should be read in conjunction with Chapter 16 which considers the financial issues relating to pension schemes, in particular 'final salary' schemes.

A stakeholder pension is of the defined contribution variety. The requirement is to offer the scheme, but not any contributions to it on behalf of employees.

Stakeholder schemes

Since 8th October 2001, employers in the UK with five or more employees (including directors) have been under a requirement to offer a 'stakeholder' pension scheme to their employees. A stakeholder pension is of the defined contribution variety (see below). The requirement is to offer the scheme, but not any contributions to it on behalf of employees. Employers can offer alternative types of schemes in lieu of a stakeholder, such as a final salary scheme, provided certain qualifying criteria are met (including certain minimum contribution levels). The stakeholder regime means that even fairly small businesses are going to have a pension scheme or arrangement of some description.

Types of pension scheme

There are different types of pension scheme. These include personal pension schemes, money purchase schemes and final salary schemes. These may in turn be tax approved or tax non-approved, funded or unfunded by the employer. It will be important at the outset to establish which type of scheme or schemes you are dealing with.

The least complicated type of scheme is a 'defined contribution' scheme. Contributions are paid by or on behalf of an employee into the scheme and the contributions are invested until he or she retires.

A 'personal pension scheme' is probably the simplest defined contribution scheme. It is a contractual arrangement made directly between the employee and the pension provider (often an insurance company).

The least complicated type of scheme is a 'defined contribution' scheme. Contributions are paid by or on behalf of an employee into the scheme and the contributions are invested until he or she retires. At that point, the accumulated fund is used to buy an annuity from an insurance company which pays a monthly or other regular amount to the pensioner until he or she dies. No particular level of benefits is guaranteed by the scheme; the annuity depends on the amount of the accumulated fund and the annuity rates which can be obtained in the market on retirement.

A 'personal pension scheme' is probably the simplest defined contribution scheme. It is a contractual arrangement made directly between the employee and the pension provider (often an insurance company). If the employee funds this himself/herself, then there is no further due diligence to be undertaken. However, if the target company has undertaken to contribute to the scheme, the purchaser should check that the contributions have been paid in a timely fashion and are not in arrears. The undertaking will usually form part of

A 'money purchase scheme' is a defined contribution scheme organized by the employer and made available to eligible employees. The scheme may or may not provide for contributions to be made by the employer in addition to any contributions made by the employee.

the employee's contract of employment and there is not much more than that to investigate.

A 'money purchase scheme' is a defined contribution scheme organized by the employer and made available to eligible employees. The scheme may or may not provide for contributions to be made by the employer in addition to any contributions made by the employee. As no particular level of benefits is guaranteed, the main concern of the purchaser will be to ensure that the company has paid all outstanding contributions and expenses to the scheme which it has undertaken to pay. Although the scheme may not itself guarantee benefits, it will be important to establish that the target company has not given any collateral undertaking to provide employees with a specific level of benefits which could ultimately represent an additional cost to the target.

A defined benefits scheme (or a final salary scheme, as it is sometimes called) undertakes to provide specific benefits to participating employees usually based on their final pay before retiring. Typically, such a scheme will provide for a pension from normal retirement age of 1/60 (or some other fraction) of final pensionable pay for each year of the employee's pensionable service. Because the scheme guarantees these benefits, it will be important to establish that the scheme has sufficient funds to provide them in the future.

> **A defined benefits scheme (or a final salary scheme, as it is sometimes called) undertakes to provide specific benefits to participating employees usually based on their final pay before retiring.**

Tax advantages

A tax-approved scheme carries a number of tax advantages. The employer is entitled to corporation tax relief on its contributions to the scheme. Participating employees are entitled to income tax relief on their own contributions and are not charged to tax on any contributions which the employer may make to the scheme for them. Income and capital gains derived from the investments of the scheme are exempt from tax. There are several conditions for approval. For instance, benefits may not exceed specified limits and it is generally a requirement for the scheme to be established under irrevocable trusts.

Final salary and money purchase schemes may be contracted out of the state earnings related pension scheme, provided the pension benefits made available under the scheme are equal to or better than the state pension. The benefit of a contracted-out scheme is that lower National Insurance contributions are payable by the employer and employees. The employer must hold a contracting-out certificate or be included in a group contracting-out certificate for the relevant scheme. A prudent purchaser will check the status of the scheme and that the correct level of National Insurance contributions are being paid.

> **The benefit of a contracted-out scheme is that lower National Insurance contributions are payable by the employer and employees.**

Equalizing benefits

It should not be forgotten that pension schemes often provide ancillary benefits. For instance, life assurance cover is commonly a feature of final salary and money purchase schemes. When considering the acquisition of a company, the potential purchaser should review all benefits, not least to ensure that, if they are more or less favourable than the benefits provided to the purchaser's own employees, proposals are in place for how to deal with the potential inequality.

Acquisition issues

In the context of an acquisition, most pension issues are likely to concern tax-approved funded schemes and in particular those schemes which offer defined benefits. The remainder of this section summarizes the issues with which a potential purchaser should be concerned.

If the target company has its own final salary scheme, one of the first things the prospective purchaser will need to do is ascertain whether the assets of the scheme are sufficient to fund fully the potential liabilities to pensioners. Such an assessment is a highly specialized matter and the purchaser will need the help of an experienced actuary to make this determination.

> **It should not be forgotten that pension schemes often provide ancillary benefits. For instance, life assurance cover is commonly a feature of final salary and money purchase schemes. The potential purchaser should review all benefits.**

As a starting point, the purchaser's actuary will wish to establish that the liabilities of the scheme towards the target's employees in respect of their period of employment up to completion of the acquisition are fully funded. In making this assessment, the actuary will wish to take into account their projected final pensionable pay at retirement as distinct from their pensionable pay as it exists at completion. This means taking account of projected pay increases after completion. Of course, the final pensionable pay will be unknown as will the future investment return on the investments of the scheme to pay for the liabilities. These are both matters which will have to be the subject of actuarial assumptions. Other assumptions will have to be made about such things as mortality rates and employees who may leave employment before retirement. There is always room for differences of opinion on the appropriate assumptions to make when assessing

whether a pension scheme is fully funded at the time of an acquisition. That is
why much will turn on the respective
views of the actuaries acting for the seller and the purchaser.

In making his assessment, the purchaser's actuary may be assisted by a
recent actuarial valuation of the scheme.
In this case, the purchaser may ask for
no more than a warranty from the seller
that the valuation is an accurate one

> **Much will turn on the respective views of the two actuaries. If there is not time to carry out a valuation prior to completion, sale agreement may provide for one to be carried out following completion.**

and that there has been no change in circumstances since it was carried out. If
a recent valuation is not available, then it may be necessary to undertake one
as part of the sale process. The question of who will pay for this will be a matter for negotiation. If the purchaser's actuary reports a shortfall in funding, this
may lead directly to a price renegotiation. The seller, of course, may resist this
particularly if advised that the actuarial assumptions applied were not reasonable ones. Again, much will turn on the respective views of the two actuaries. If
there is not time to carry out a valuation prior to completion, the sale agreement may provide for one to be carried out following completion. The method of
valuation and the actuarial assumptions to be applied will be a matter for
detailed negotiation in the sale agreement. To the extent that the valuation
shows a shortfall in funding, the agreement would provide for a retrospective
adjustment of the purchase price.

If the scheme has surplus funding, the seller may wish this to be taken into
account in the purchase price. The purchaser should be cautious about this however because, without getting into the technicalities, there can be restrictions on
extracting a surplus from a continuing pension scheme or otherwise taking
advantage of it by future contribution holidays. Detailed legal and actuarial
advice will be needed to determine to what extent the price can be fairly
increased to take account of the surplus.

If the target company is one of a number of companies participating in a
group pension scheme then, unless it is the principal employer, it will have to
withdraw from that scheme on or following completion. In these circumstances,
it is usually agreed that a transfer payment will be made from the group
scheme to a new scheme for the benefit of the target company's employees. The
purchaser will wish to ensure that the transfer payment is sufficient to fund
the pension liabilities of those employees in the same way as if it were the target's own scheme. It will also wish to make sure that there are no continuing
liabilities of the target company in connection with the group scheme.

Where a transfer payment is to be made to a new scheme, the sale agreement is likely to set out in detail the basis on which the transfer payment will be made and the actuarial assumptions which will be applied to calculate it. It should be remembered, however, that where the pension scheme is established under irrevocable trusts, it is the trustees who must independently consider the correct transfer payment to be made and that is not a matter over which the seller and the purchaser have control. The sale agreement is likely to say that the seller will use his reasonable endeavours to persuade the trustees to make a payment on the agreed basis but that if a sum less than this or, indeed, more than this is eventually transferred, then the purchase price for the target company will be retrospectively adjusted to compensate for this.

A purchaser should consider whether the pension scheme is discriminatory in any fashion. Pension schemes have suffered in the past from discriminating against one of the sexes or against part time workers.

Finally, a purchaser should consider whether the pension scheme is discriminatory in any fashion. Pension schemes have suffered in the past from discriminating against one of the sexes or against part time workers. The purchaser should seek advice as to whether there are any potential liabilities in this respect and whether these necessitate a price adjustment or appropriate indemnities to protect the purchaser.

Scope of the pre-acquisition due diligence report

Introduction

This section will contain an introduction to the report, including:

- The terms of reference
- Scope of the work, including any limitations
- Basis of information within the report
- Verification of factual accuracy
- Access to key personnel

Summary of findings

A concise summary of the contents of the report and the principal findings of the investigation

History and commercial activities

Provides a brief description of the history and development of the business and its current operation:

- Details of the legal structure of the business and its ownership
- The business's current strategies with reference to the latest business plan or corporate brochures
- A summary history of the business including key events in its development and its current strategies
- An analysis of turnover and gross margin by product/service, geographical market and major customer for the last three completed financial years
- A description of the following areas:

    (a) Activities and products or services, including new products or services which have been recently introduced or are planned

    (b) Industry, markets and competition, including an assessment (where possible) of the size and development of the principal markets in which the business operates, its market share and its strengths and weaknesses *vis-à-vis* its competitors, barriers to entry

(c) Customers and marketing, including terms of trade with customers, contracts with customers, pricing policy, gross margins, details of sales and marketing operations, marketing strategy, distribution channels, guarantees and warranty terms, quality policy

(d) Suppliers and production, including extent of reliance on key suppliers, contracts and terms of trade with suppliers

- A description of the business locations including the nature of tenure
- Details of any legal agreements or actions affecting the group

Organization structure and employees

Summarizes the details of the management structure and senior managers, together with the key characteristics of the workforce, highlighting strengths, weaknesses and constraining factors:

- A description of the management and reporting structure of the business
- Details of the management and senior employees of the business, covering their roles, experience and terms of employment including remuneration package, length of service and service contracts
- Identification of the key personnel and succession plans
- Details for other employees of:
  (a) Current staffing levels in each area of operation and any proposed changes, details of staff turnover rates and any difficulties in recruitment
  (b) Salary/wage structure, terms of employment including holidays, pensions and other benefits, notice period, etc.
  (c) Dates of salary/wage reviews and current status of such
  (d) Details of profit sharing and bonus schemes
  (e) Recruitment and training policies
  (f) The extent of unionisation and commentary on any major disputes arising during the period of review and staff relations in general
- Identification of any important relationships with outside contractors and professional advisers and the extent of the business's reliance upon them
- Details of pension schemes and an indication of their funding positions

Accounting policies and audit issues

Considers the acceptability of key accounting policies and practices:

- A commentary on the accounting policies adopted by the business and their detailed implementation, including compliance with UK GAAP. Details of any changes in policy during the review period
- Identification of accounting policies that differ from those of the company and an assessment of the impact of restating the target's results using the company's policies
- Details of the policy adopted in respect of the recognition of turnover and any other undisclosed policies and practices
- A review of the auditors' working papers, commenting specifically on any control weaknesses identified in management letters and any adjustments made to management accounts to arrive at year end audited accounts

Management information and internal control

Provides an overview of the substance and adequacy of management information and internal controls:

- A review of key management information prepared by the business
- A review of the structure of, and responsibilities within, the finance function
- Details of the key internal controls operated by the business and the frequency, basis of preparation, and reliability of management accounts, including the reasonableness of any general assumptions made in their preparation
- A brief overview of the accounting and operational computer systems used by the business including, as appropriate:

  (a) Hardware and operating systems

  (b) Software used commenting on the extent of bespoke software

  (c) Redundancy and robustness

  (d) Service, support and upgrade arrangements and contracts

  (e) Disaster recovery and backup procedures

- To the extent that the above procedure identifies systems weaknesses or other issues, a discussion on the scope of any additional work that may be appropriate should take place

Trading results

Explains and comments on the significant factors behind the reported trading results for recent years and any exceptional or non-recurring items which have had a material impact:

- A summary of the historical results of the business covering the latest available three-year period (the 'review period')
- An explanation of the major fluctuations in turnover and profits during the review period, to identify seasonality and industry trends
- A breakdown of gross profit analysed by each main activity for the review period together with an explanation as to significant variations
- An analysis of overhead expenses together with comments on significant fluctuations
- A summary of intragroup trading and any related party transactions
- An explanation of, and comments on, trends disclosed by the results to include relevant notes of any exceptional profits or losses and any other significant contributory factors

Assets and liabilities

Explains and comments on the assets and liabilities of the business and, in particular, considers valuation bases and the basis of recognizing liabilities:

- A summary of the balance sheets of the business during the review period and at the latest management accounts date
- A commentary and analysis of the principal balance sheet items, including:
  - (a) Tangible fixed assets, to include an analysis of the net book value of fixed assets by category, a commentary on capitalisation, revaluation and depreciation policies and details of capital expenditure, current capital commitments and any grants received
  - (b) Stock, to include the basis of valuation, method of provisioning and stock turnover
  - (c) Debtors, to include the basis of bad debt provisioning and bad debt history, ageing of debtors, debtor days and commentary on the adequacy or otherwise of the bad debt and credit note provisions
  - (d) Creditors, to include hire purchase/finance lease commitments, details of accruals and deferred income

(e) Details of bank facilities and security provided, and details of any penalty clauses included in the facilities agreement for withdrawing from such arrangements

(f) Details of any off-balance sheet financing

(g) Provisions for liabilities and charges, to include deferred taxation, the basis of providing for warranty costs and recent claims history

(h) Details of any contingent liabilities

Cash flows

Summarizes recent cash flow patterns and the significant factors affecting cash flow:

- A summary of the cash flow statements of the business during the review period
- An analysis of the cash flow statements and major cash flow movements, including appropriate commentary thereon
- Details of any seasonality in cash flow

Current trading

Summarizes and comments on trading results for the period since the last completed financial period:

- A review and commentary on the results shown by the latest management accounts, comparing them with budgeted results for the period and actual results for the corresponding period in the previous financial year

Financial projections

Comments on management's trading and cash flow projections, the method of their compilation, and key underlying assumptions, with particular reference to their relationship with current trading levels:

- A description of budgeting procedures, including a commentary on management's review process and past experience in budgeting
- A summary of the profit and cash flow projections of the business
- A review of the profit and cash flow projections of the business for a period to be agreed, including the following:

  (a) A review of the projections' arithmetical accuracy

  (b) A review of the assumptions made by the directors and comments upon any assumptions that appear unrealistic with respect to past performance

(c) A review of cash flow projections against borrowing facilities

(d) A sensitivity analysis of the projections in relation to the key assumptions upon which they have been prepared

Taxation

Summarizes details of the current status of the tax affairs of the business:

- A summary of the tax affairs of the business, including:

  (a) A review of the most recent corporation tax computations for which either (i) an agreed assessment has been issued, or (ii) the period permitted under corporation tax self-assessment for the tax authorities to raise enquiries has ended; or (iii) for which a notice of closure in respect of a corporation tax self-assessment enquiry has been issued

  (b) A commentary on the effective rate of taxation

  (c) A summary of agreed tax and ACT losses, if any, and their likely future offset

  (d) A review of 'open' returns submitted to the tax authorities including a commentary on any queries raised by them

  (e) A discussion of the reasons for any delays in submitting/agreeing tax computations and any resultant fines and penalties paid or due

  (f) A review of the results of the last VAT inspection

  (g) A review of the results of the last PAYE/NIC inspections

  (h) A review of any recent reconstructions, reorganisations and tax clearance applications

Standard information checklist for a financial due diligence investigation

The review period would typically cover the last three years

History and commercial activities

- Summary of the legal structure and ownership of and any changes since the last annual return

- Brief account of history, locations and nature of business

- Copy of the latest business plan and/or any corporate brochures

- Description of products/services and any other trading activities

- Details of main competitors and market position, including estimated market share and any recent industry surveys

- Details of key customers including terms of trade and an analysis of turnover by customer during the review period

- Details of key suppliers including terms of trade and an analysis of purchases by supplier during the review period

- Particulars of any long-term agreements with customers or suppliers and any other significant agreements, contracts or arrangements with third parties

- Note of alternative arrangements for important supplies which are currently single sourced

- Production methods and techniques and the relative position of the business in relation to the 'state of the art' in the industry in which it operates

- Summary of premises showing locations, facilities/area, tenure and purpose, premises not currently in use and the availability of any spare land or buildings

- Details of any rent payable or receivable and sight of leases or tenancy agreements including details of any onerous lease provisions

- Details of any intellectual property and whether the target has taken steps to protect it
- Details of any litigation
- Copies of all contracts relating to the acquisition or disposal of companies or businesses during the last six years

Organization structure and employees

- Summary of the management structure and division of responsibilities
- List of directors and senior executives and particulars as to:
  - previous experience and connection before joining business
  - formal qualifications
  - duties throughout the review period
  - age, years of service and date of appointment to the board, if applicable
  - current remuneration
  - pension arrangements
  - other benefits (e.g. use of company car)
  - service agreements
  - directorships of companies that carry on business of any kind with the target or its subsidiaries
- Names of former directors and senior executives who have left during the review period along with reasons for departure
- Analysis of staff by department or function and an indication of staff turnover levels
- Details of key employees and the strategies to retain them
- Description of salary/wage structure, terms of employment including holidays, pensions and other benefits, notice period, etc.
- Details of recent and imminent salary/wage reviews
- Description of recruitment and training policies
- Names of active trades unions, if any, and number of staff affiliated to each
- Details of any disputes during the review period and current staff relations in general
- Details of relationships with self-employed staff, external consultants, contractors and professional advisers

- Details of any restrictive covenants placed on staff who have recently joined or left the company.
- Details of any pension and share option schemes.

Accounting policies and audit issues

- Copies of audit management letters for the review period
- Authority from the target's auditors to allow access to their working papers for the review period

Management information and control systems

- Details of the IT systems architecture (including web, ERP and accounting systems), the interfaces between each and the extent to which each is used for the reporting of financial and non-financial operating data
- Details of back-up and disaster recovery procedures
- Details of the management information reporting process, including the consolidation process where applicable
- Details of the budget setting process and results of previous comparisons to actual results
- Summary of the key internal controls in place

Trading results

Where possible the following analyses should be provided on a monthly basis:

- Copies of financial statements produced during the review period including interim and non-statutory accounts, if any
- Analysis of turnover and gross profit by principle product groups, customers and geographic destination for the review period
- Analysis of overheads by nature
- Management accounts and other management information used in monitoring the business for the review period, with a reconciliation to the financial statements
- Details of any special features which have influenced the trading results in any year
- Details of any intragroup or related party transactions
- Details of any currency exposure and hedging arrangements

Assets and liabilities

The following analyses need only be provided at year ends in the first instance:

- Description of fixed asset capitalization, revaluation and depreciation policies
- Sight of any recent independent or internal valuations
- Analysis of valuation, cost, depreciation/amortization and net book value of fixed assets by major category, age and whether owned or leased for the review period
- Details of grants received, capital commitments and any significant capital expenditure anticipated but not contracted for
- Analysis of stock (gross and net of any provisions), including ageing and method of valuation
- Analysis of debtors (gross and net of any provisions) by nature and age
- Analysis of creditors by nature and age and a description of their repayment bases
- Details of hire purchase, leasing and rental agreements
- Details of loan or overdraft facilities, security provided, interest and repayment terms and any penalty clauses stipulated for withdrawing from such agreements
- Details of any warranty liabilities and recent claims history
- Details of any contingent, off-balance sheet financing or other liabilities not covered above

Cash flows

- Cash flow statements for the review period if not included in the financial statements
- An explanation of the major variances in the net cash position over the review period

Financial projections

- Any budgets, forecasts and projections available
- Description of basis on which the projections have been derived and supporting evidence where available

Current trading

- Monthly management accounts since the review period
- Analysis of the management accounts in line with that provided for the review period, including a commentary on variances to budget

Taxation

- Tax computations and sight of correspondence covering the review period
- Details of current status of tax computations and disputes with tax authorities
- Analysis of brought forward tax losses and ACT, if any, by date of creation.
- Sight of any apportionment clearances which have been obtained
- Summary of the findings of the most recent VAT and PAYE/NIC inspections
- Details of any reconstructions, reorganizations and tax clearances during the review period

Other

- Copies of any circulars to members
- Sight of minute books, other statutory books and of the memorandum and articles of association

Checklist for legal due diligence

Constitution/ownership/status

- Up-to-date constitutional document
  - Does the corporate vendor have power to sell its shares in target?
  - Are there any restrictions in target's articles to the transfer of shares?
- Details of the authorized and issued share capital
- Details of shareholders (including capacity in which they hold shares and any dissenting or untraceable shareholders)
- Shareholders' agreements (if any)
- Organizational chart identifying target's group structure and current directors of each group entity
- Options or encumbrances over target's share capital?
- Are any assets used by target owned otherwise than by target?
- Are any of target's assets encumbered or other than in its possession?
- Are any of the vendors or persons closely connected to them party to or interested in or entitled to any contracts, loans, intellectual property rights, assets, competitive business or claims of, to, by, against or used by target?

Main contracts

- Copies of all manufacturing joint venture, partnership, agency, distributorship, licensing, supply, franchising, out-sourcing agreements and standard contracts for sale of goods/supply of services
- Is target solvent? Are any insolvency proceedings pending?
- Details of all major customers and suppliers
  - Any adverse change in relationships?
- Copies of all contracts relating to target's sale/purchase of companies/business/assets in last six years
- Copies of loan/credit agreements and related security/guarantee documentation
- Bank account details and mandates
  - Does the acquisition require bank's consent?

- Details of any major option or right exercisable on change of control of target
- Detail of non-compliance with any contracts
- Is target a party to any non-arm's length arrangement?
- Has target given a guarantee or indemnity of any third party's obligations?
- Are any of target's contracts subject to avoidance under insolvency legislation?
- Any contracts dependent on compliance with British Standards or other special accreditations.

Accounts/financial position

- Audited accounts for last three years
- Any management/internal accounts prepared subsequently
- Other documents relating to the financial/trading position of the target since last accounting date
  - Accountants' report?
- Any material adverse change since date of audited accounts?
- Any bad or doubtful debts?
- Are stocks adequate, excessive, unusuable, etc?
- Is target's plant and equipment in good condition/does it need replacement?
- Has target received any grant?
  - Is this liable to repayment?
  - Can it be forfeited?
- Any expenses borne by target other than for the benefit of target?

Property

- Schedule of properties
- Purchaser to investigate title or vendor's solicitors to issue certificate of title?
- Copies of all deeds and other documents necessary to prove good title
- Copies of all insurance policies
- Details of any mortgages, charges, leases, tenancies, options, licences, restrictive covenants, easements or other restrictions or rights affecting the properties
- Details of all property outgoings

- Details of any disputes with adjoining owners (actual or pending)
- Surveyors' reports?
- Planning/use restrictions?
- Necessary planning permissions/building regulation approvals obtained?
- Special risks (e.g. mines, flooding, subsidence, landfill, common land, asbestos, deleterious materials, environmental etc.)
- Any contingent liabilities under previously assigned leases?

Employment and pensions

- Copies of all standard terms and conditions of employment and details of material deviations
- Identify key employees
  - What is their likely response to the sale?
  - What would be their value to the target post acquisition?
- Details of all directors' service agreements (in particular salaries, notice periods, restrictive covenants and 'parachute' provisions)
- Details of any bonus/profit sharing/option schemes for directors/employees
- Identify all existing and potential employee claims against target
- Details of all pension schemes (including actuarial valuations)
  - What are employer's obligations?

Intellectual property rights

- Identify all registered IPRs and conduct necessary searches (i.e. Trade Marks Registry, Patents Office)
- Identify all material unregistered IPRs
- Particulars of any licence agreement granted by or to a third party
- Details of any IPR-related disputes (actual or prospective)
- Particulars of all confidentiality agreements to which the target is party
- Does target trade under any name other than its full corporate name?
  - Is it protected?

Information technology

- Is the processing of any of target's data under the control of any third party?
- Do target's computer systems have adequate capacity for the foreseeable future?
- What disaster recover plans are in place?
- Is any third-party software subject to appropriate escrow arrangements?
- Has target suffered any material breakdowns in respect of its computer systems?
- Does target have adequate backup, security and anti-virus protection?
- Is target properly licensed to use the software it actually uses?
- Is any of target's software subject to a 'time stamp' or 'logic bomb' or 'date field' or similar restrictions?

Taxation

- Details for the last six years of all target/target group tax returns and any prior year still open
- Any intragroup transfer of capital assets in last six years?
- Any tax liabilities incurred since date of last audited accounts other than in the ordinary course of trading?

Miscellaneous

- Any other relevant insurance arrangements (product liability/recall, etc.)?
- Any current claims under insurance policies?
  - Are any policies liable to be avoided?
- Particulars of any other existing or threatened litigation or claims
- Contingent liabilities? (e.g. product liability, guarantees, maintenance obligations, product returns, liabilities under customer incentives, etc.)
- Overseas subsidiaries: what overseas advice is required? What governmental or tax consents are required?

Key secondary information sources for company, market and country information

This is not meant to be exhaustive, but should serve as a basic checklist for the secondary information sources that are available for the following subject areas: company information, market information, and national-level information.

Company information

Company reports

Available from corporate websites. Also, a searchable directory of company reports available online can be found at:

www.carol.co.uk/index.html – coverage is global, for listed companies.

National registers of companies/company accounts (Companies House and equivalent organizations overseas)

Companies House *www.companieshouse.gov.uk/info/* – for basic, free information, for downloadable full company accounts, use Companies House Direct (*www.direct.companies-house.gov.uk/*)

Equivalent organizations in other European countries include the:

- ORT (France) – *www.ort.fr*
- Camerdata (Spain) – *www.camerdata.es* – but it is expensive and troublesome to access full reports.

The FAME/AMADEUS databases, both in the British Library, provide company financials for the UK and Europe as a whole respectively.

Publicly listed US companies are listed on the Edgarscan site:

edgarscan.pwcglobal.com/servlets/edgarscan

News sources

Reuters Business Briefing includes company information and financial information.

www.findarticles.com includes company information and it is free and comprehensive.

The FT remains an important news source: *www.ft.com*; *www.globalarchive.ft.com*

A further good source of free information is *www.individual.com*

Investment or brokerage reports

Investment or brokerage reports are prepared by analysts at brokerage houses and investment banks. They provide information on individual companies as well as on the markets within which these companies operate. They also provide some comparisons of the performance of a specific company to that of its key competitors. Sites which carry investment reports include:

- Reuters Business Briefing (see website above): accessing broker reports will incur additional charges on top of the pay-per-minute rate;
- Hoovers (11 million reports available) (*www.hoovers.com /*);
- Thomson Financial (Research bank and Venture X databases): sources include more than 800 investment banks, market research firms, and trade associations worldwide encompassing 2.5 million reports offering coverage over 40,000 companies (public and private) in over 85 countries.
- Exclusive reports from CSFB, Salomon Smith Barney, DataQuest and Simba;
- Datastar (*www.datastar.com*) and Multex (*www.multexinvestor.com*) are aggregators of reports, similar to Thomson and Reuters;
- Northern Light: search engine has broker and market reports within its 'special collections' section.

Business school case studies

Business school case studies are potential sources of historic company information, and on industrial sectors.

A searchable directory of business cases is provided by Cranfield University (*www.ecch.cranfield.ac.uk /*). This covers Harvard Business School, INSEAD and a number of other reputable business schools.

Market information

Competitive intelligence/business intelligence directory sites

Competitor intelligence resources and links lists: *www.fuld.com*

Archive/forum for business information professionals: *www.freepint.co.uk*

Excellent portal for business information: *www.dis.strath.ac.uk / business /*

Market research reports

A directory of market research reports can be found at *www.mindbranch.com*

The major consultancy firms also publish overviews of markets/ industries (or 'white papers') on their websites.

Market research reports are available to buy on a page by page basis from *www.northernlight.com*

Market research companies

A list of market research companies and a brief description of their main specialisms can be found at the following sites:

- *www.dis.strath.ac.uk / business / marketres.html*
- *www.irn-research.com*

Trade Associations/professional bodies

A listing of British Trade Associations is provided at: *www.martex.co.uk / taf / index.htm*

It is also worth checking out the library and information resources offered by trade associations.

Trade Publications

Willing's publications guide and *Benn's Media* provide a comprehensive list of all publications.

An online list of publications can be found at: *www.publist.com*

Industry experts

Academic research centres are listed at:
www.niss.ac.uk/education/hefc/rae96/c1_96.html

This lists all UK academic departments, by subject area, with a rating of their research records, which can be used as a proxy measure for 'expertise'.

Key academics in social sciences and their research areas can be found at: *www.regard.ac.uk/regard/home/index_html*

This is a database of research funded by the Economic and Social Research Council, searchable by subject.

Subscribing to email discussion groups and trawling their archives or posting provocative questions may unearth experts. Searchable directories of email discussion guides can be found at:

- *www.liszt.com*

- *www.lsoft.com/ lists/ listref.html*

Trade shows

Exhibitor lists are particularly useful as a means of identifying companies. Directories of trade shows can be found at:

- *www.exhibitions.co.uk/catlist.html*
- *www.tsnn.co.uk/*
- *www.expobase.com*

National-level information

A directory of UK government departments is provided at:
www.open.gov.uk/

The website of the Office of National Statistics is also a valuable source of data: *www.statistics.gov.uk/statbase*

All UK government documentation (paper) can be searched at:
www.parliament.the-stationery-office.co.uk/cgi-bin/empower?DB=ukparl

A directory of online government information for countries outside the UK can be found at: *www.gksoft.com/govt*

A directory of links to official statistics of countries outside the UK is available at: *www.auckland.ac.nz/lbr/stats/offstats/OFFSTATSmain.htm*

Basic statistics on countries are available from:

- *www.corporateinformation.com* (it has good links to country-specific information sources)

- *www.exportall.com*

- *www.dis.strath.ac.uk / business / countries.html*

  European statistical data is available from:
  www.europa.eu.int / index_en.htm

Index

225